Advance Praise for

"Reading *Halfway Home* feels like having a conversation with a very wise, witty friend. Christina Myers's delightful collection of essays about the stages of a woman's life is personal, but also universal. We've all been there, and it's a joy to realize that we're not alone on the journey." —Elizabeth Renzetti, author of *Shrewed: A Wry and Closely Observed Look at the Lives of Women and Girls*

"Christina Myers effortlessly charts the often-overlooked territory of being a woman in today's complex society. Through insightful personal essays, she explores the intricate intersections of femininity, friendship, motherhood, and environmental turbulence, all with a nostalgic flair. With much-needed humour and wisdom, Myers reminds us that even in the midst of uncertainty, we're never alone on this journey. This book is a necessary, heartfelt guide for those seeking their own unique path through the maze of midlife. A must read!" —Chelene Knight, award-winning author of *Let It Go: Free Yourself from Old Beliefs and Find a New Path to Joy*

"From the wise vantage point of mid-age, Christina Myers has located a voice ringing with clarity—a writer who finally trusts her own instincts. Those who fondly remember the candy sweetness of Love's Baby Soft will be charmed by these rite-of-passage essays. When girl- and womanhood can feel lonely, *Halfway Home* reminds us of the universal aspects we share and that 'there wasn't anything wrong with us in the first place.' Looking back, looking forward, and looking down at the miraculous bodies that have carried us here, this warm and insightful collection of ruminations confirms that our lives, with all of their bumps, swerves, and surprises, are valuable." —Tara McGuire, former broadcaster and author of *Holden After and Before: Love Letter for a Son Lost to Overdose*

"Christina Myers's essays are bewitching in their insight and exhilarating in their clear-eyed examination of the oppressive systems that seek to crush and contain women. With tenderness and gleeful moments of discovery, *Halfway Home* begins a map that readers and the author create together, finding a way forward in a strange new world where traditional paths for women lead nowhere and new ones are still being cleared." —Hollay Ghadery, award-winning author of *Fuse*

"*Halfway Home* is a love letter to mothers and grandmothers, sisters and daughters, witches and crones. Christina Myers's storytelling is gentle and honest, a must-read memoir for women of all ages. So many times, I found myself nodding and exclaiming, 'Yes! That's exactly it!' It's a mirror but also an invitation to join a secret coven of wise women." —K. J. Aiello, author of *The Monster and the Mirror: Mental Illness, Magic, and the Stories We Tell*

"*Halfway Home* is a gracefully written exploration of what it means to be a woman in a complicated world, navigating the terrain from first bras and first periods to hot flashes and perimenopause and the uncharted landscape beyond. Christina Myers offers up a warm-hearted, absorbing read that you'll want to devour in one sitting and return to in quiet moments with a cup of tea and a box of tissues as you laugh-cry your way through essays that make you want to shout out loud in solidarity. In sharing her own journey with honesty, vulnerability, and insight, Myers invites you to extend compassion to the younger self you once were and to embrace the flawed beauty of the crone you are becoming. This is a book that demands to be shared with all the wise women in your own world—sisters, mothers, daughters, friends—as it reminds you of the truth we all need to hear: Amidst all the messiness, chaos, and unravelling that comes along with midlife, you are not, and never will be, alone." —Julie MacLellan, former arts and culture editor and journalist

"These clever, articulate, powerful true stories explore many issues relevant to midlife: the misinformation we carry from childhood, 'the gospel of worthiness,' 'the doctrine of the make-over,' the sacred knowledge of women, and more. Most of all, the author deals with the need to belong, including as a mother, a sexual being, [and] a feminist ... readers rooting for this lively, fiercely honest writer will be happy that Christina Myers finds her way home." —Beth Kaplan, author of *Midlife Solo: Writing through Chaos to Find My Place in the World*

"As I run around looking like a hot mess—where my body and mind change, disappoint, and introduce themselves anew each year—I need *Halfway Home* for my own survival. As Christina Myers writes, the old maps are no longer reliable. Friends, leggings, growing children, and forms, she makes me laugh, cry, shiver, hold my breath, and sigh, inspiring a conversation with

my younger, present, and future self. What are the big brown envelopes we carry with us over the decades? What myths have we swallowed whole that we struggle to break free? How do we measure ourselves, time, and (mid)life itself? *Halfway Home* reminds me to let go of the 'aspirational impossibilities' and welcome in the things we have been systematically 'taught to forget.' Myers reminds me I get to decide how to live this one midlife. Let her see you, so you too can see yourself through."
—Carys Cragg, author of *Dead Reckoning: How I Came to Meet the Man Who Murdered My Father*, finalist for the Governor General's Literary Award for Non-Fiction

"Compulsively readable, Christina Myers's *Halfway Home: Thoughts from Midlife* is the tour through life that every Gen X woman never knew she needed. From Sears training bras, sneaking tampons into the ladies' room, and makeover magazines, to being forced to wear a too-tight employee uniform T-shirt before the rise of the #MeToo movement, Myers has seen it all, as she mothers teenagers who do and don't need her anymore, allowing sapphire-blue leggings to transform her life. Let this midlife new best friend lovingly guide you through your anti-wrinkle cream, perimenopause, and climate change uncertainties. Grieving all the other lives we might have had, Myers prepares us to move into our wisest years yet, where a woman past her prime isn't less than what she was before: instead, she is more. I would follow her anywhere." —Catherine Lewis, author of *Zipless*

Halfway Home

Thoughts from Midlife

Christina Myers

ANANSI

Published in Canada in 2024 and the USA in 2024 by House of Anansi Press Inc.
houseofanansi.com

House of Anansi Press is committed to protecting our natural environment. This book is made of material from well-managed FSC®-certified forests, recycled materials, and other controlled sources.

House of Anansi Press is a Global Certified Accessible™ (GCA by Benetech) publisher. The ebook version of this book meets stringent accessibility standards and is available to readers with print disabilities.

28 27 26 25 24   1 2 3 4 5

Library and Archives Canada Cataloguing in Publication
Title: Halfway home : thoughts from midlife / Christina Myers.
Names: Myers, Christina, author.
Identifiers: Canadiana (print) 20230596878 | Canadiana (ebook) 20230597149 |
ISBN 9781487012441 (softcover) | ISBN 9781487012458 (EPUB)
Subjects: LCSH: Myers, Christina. | LCSH: Middle age—Psychological aspects. | LCSH: Middle-aged women. | LCSH: Middle-aged persons. | LCGFT: Autobiographies. | LCGFT: Creative nonfiction.
Classification: LCC BF724.6 .M94 2024 | DDC 155.6/6—dc23

Cover design: Jennifer Lum
Cover image: Iryna Reshetniak @ iStock
Book design/Typesetting: Lucia Kim

House of Anansi Press is grateful for the privilege to work on and create from the Traditional Territory of many Nations, including the Anishinabeg, the Wendat, and the Haudenosaunee, as well as the Treaty Lands of the Mississaugas of the Credit.

 Canada Council   Conseil des Arts
for the Arts   du Canada

 ONTARIO ARTS COUNCIL
CONSEIL DES ARTS DE L'ONTARIO
an Ontario government agency
un organisme du gouvernement de l'Ontario

With the participation of the Government of Canada | Canadä
Avec la participation du gouvernement du Canada

We acknowledge for their financial support of our publishing program the Canada Council for the Arts, the Ontario Arts Council, and the Government of Canada.

Printed and bound in Canada

MIX
Paper from
responsible sources
FSC® C103567

To the sisters, the mothers, the daughters, the bosom friends, the crones, the witches, the wise women, the weirdos: thank you. I could not have survived without you.

"Nothing is absolute. Everything changes, everything moves, everything revolves, everything flies and goes away."
—Frida Kahlo

Contents

Introduction

While I was writing this book, people would ask from time to time what exactly I was writing about. Oh, I would say, well, it's about a lot of things: being a woman, having a body, mothering. It's about aging and wrinkles and periods and menopause and fat phobia. Oh, and witchcraft. Sex. And climate change. The end of the world. Beauty standards. And did I mention bodies? I'd ramble on and on, touching on this theme and that, sharing the ideas and concepts I was attempting to explore. Then I'd say: yeah, it's kind of a mix of all of that, really.

They'd blink in confusion, tilt their heads, frown.

I've always been terrible at the elevator pitch—I can only explain to you what a book is about if the elevator breaks down and we have a half hour to hash it out. If you need me to tell you before we get to the tenth floor, I'm in trouble.

But after enough rounds of attempting to describe what I was working on, and being met by the confused blink-and-frown, I eventually learned to cap my synopsis by saying: "It's really about midlife, about being in midlife, about being a woman right now in this time, and about looking back at where I've come from and looking ahead to, well, whatever is ahead. All of the uncertainty that lives there—and learning, maybe, to be comfortable with that uncertainty."

Ah! This made more sense to people. Their eyes would light up in understanding. Yes, yes, of course, midlife. A simple shorthand anyone could understand because everyone exists in some relation to midlife: you are past it already, living in it right now, or aware that it is coming (in that vague hypothetical way we all seem to have about the idea of time passing when we are too young to have really felt it yet).

But then would come the same, inevitable question: Aren't you too young to be writing about that?

So deeply steeped am I in our culture's fear of aging and its parallel worship of youth, that for a split second, I'd be flattered and pleased by this question. Oh, well, thank you very much, I'd say. Then I'd stop and remind myself what this observation really meant. I've often been told I look younger than I am, and I'd always heard this as a compliment. But now I was hearing it as a prohibition against what mattered most to me: figuring out where I was, how I got here, and who I am, in the only way I've ever figured out anything in my life—by writing about it.

So I'd say no, I don't think I'm too young. I don't think I'm too young at all. I'd announce my age: well north of forty-five, close to fifty before this book might be done. I'm Generation X, I'd point out, and the *New York Times* is already writing about the "millennial middle-age experience."

Depending on who I was talking to, I'd throw in that I was a mother to *teenagers*, or that I was now in the *annual mammogram* stage of life. Sometimes I'd crack jokes about perimenopause, or point to this deep vertical wrinkle on my forehead that I've had since my twenties, or announce with great enthusiasm, "I just got progressive lenses!" I'd tell them that in *The Golden Girls*, the younger three characters were meant to be in their early fifties. Surely *they* were deemed well into midlife—or, in fact, beyond it?

Sometimes the person I was talking to would seem convinced, but not always. Someone born the same year as me could either agree wholeheartedly about where we were in life, or be vehemently opposed, based on their own comfort with, or fear of, aging and the stereotypes they've absorbed about midlife and what's beyond it. The truth is we're hard-pressed to determine exactly what midlife is, and everyone seems to have their own definition, relative to where they're standing themselves.

Many of us think of midlife as a time marked by the physical: hot flashes in the middle of the night, the first grey hairs. Our bodies change in myriad ways, most of which we don't celebrate and many that we actively try to fix or hide.

Still others will say you'll know you're in it when you have your midlife crisis, which apparently includes buying a sports car, or having an affair with someone much younger, or getting a facelift, or any number of equally clichéd Hollywood options. This seems rather like claiming that the way to know you're riding a bike is if there's a loaf of French bread sticking out of the basket. Just because it appears in films an awful lot doesn't make it true.

Some people mark midlife by age, of course, though what age exactly is always a tricky calculation. Midlife researchers tend to focus on the forty-to-sixty range, but that seems flexible, too.

Deep down, I don't think any of us really come to find ourselves in midlife by noticing wrinkles or hitting a certain age or driving that red convertible. I believe midlife is the point at which you realize—sometimes in a moment of singular clarity, sometimes in slow, progressive steps—that your time is finite. Not just as a sentiment or idea, but as a physical reality. There will be no do-over, and no chance to rewind, erase, and start fresh. This is it, Buckaroo. One and done.

In retrospect, my midlife revelation began a few days after my fortieth birthday, when I found myself in a hospital emergency room having a major health crisis despite feeling the best I had since my teens in the months prior. As I lay there hooked up to beeping machines, I realized that I was already several years beyond the halfway point of my father's life span; he had died at sixty-seven.

A few years later, my oldest child became a teenager.

Overnight, he was stronger than me, taller than me, faster than me. His younger sister was not far behind. No one needed me to tie shoes or hold hands at the crosswalk anymore. The midlife clock ticked a little closer.

Then, lying in bed one night a few months after the start of the pandemic, I texted a friend: *Can't sleep. Is this insomnia, COVID anxiety, or just garden-variety existential dread about the state of the world?*

She replied: *Yes. All of them. And perimenopause.*

Perimenopause? This had not occurred to me. Despite a lifetime of fearing this looming monster, and being in the right age group, it had not dawned on me until that moment that this was going to happen to me. But it *was* going to happen to me. In fact, it had already begun.

I had arrived at midlife station, right on schedule.

For millennia, humans mostly lived in ways that replicated prior generations. This is the time of year to hunt. This is where to find berries in the right season. Here's how you grind wheat and here's how you make bread from it. This is your role as a child, as a parent, as an elder. We knew what to expect in the future. The world changed, of course, but the arc of that change was glacial. It might take a dozen generations, maybe a hundred, for things in day-to-day life to shift dramatically.

Now it takes only a single generation for the world to become a different place with new expectations and assumptions. The world I was born into in the mid-1970s—when lots of people still had black-and-white televisions and a single rotary phone in the kitchen—is gone. The era of forty-year jobs followed by decent pensions has ended, unless you're a teacher or a nurse (and you're lucky if you don't burn out in those careers and quit early). Women are expected to be both grandmothers and sexpots; Jennifer Lopez is fifty-four, as of this writing, and she was on the cover of a magazine I saw in the grocery lineup this week in a bikini, an aspirational impossibility. Every few days we learn of another species gone extinct, or read about car tires melting on the concrete in a record-breaking heat wave.

I can't take my cues for how to move forward into the next part of my life from my mother or my grandmother, because the worlds we inhabited during this phase of our lives are too different. The Golden Girls were not pondering how their children might live in a world facing mass extinctions and natural disasters from climate change. Nor were they wondering how they might ever retire, living with historic inflation and a wild housing market while watching their health care system and the social net unravel. Life has changed and, with it, midlife has changed, too; it continues to change at an unprecedented pace.

Of course, the world is also different in good ways. I can divorce my husband if I need to, and I can get my own credit card and bank account. I can vote for whoever I'd like. I can run for office and others can vote for me. I can access safe abortions for myself (though it's unlikely at this point I'd need it) or for my daughter. I can talk about abuse if I experience it and people will (hopefully) believe me. I can skip church my entire life and not go to jail for it. Heck, I can openly celebrate Yule without being burned at the stake. I don't have to behave, or be proper. I can have rainbow hair at any age.

I wouldn't trade the progress of this era for the slow-evolving certainty of earlier ones. But the changes means that all the old reliable maps don't quite make sense anymore. The path for my generation is not well-worn yet, and only some of the old trails are still passable. I'm trudging through a forest that has no guidebook. I'm half-way home, and I don't know the rest of the route.

My default setting tends to be one of optimism and cheer-fulness. I am lucky in this, it seems to me. Life is hard, full of days you wish you could undo, choices you didn't want to make, and people you will never get to see again. Your heart will be broken over and over; mine certainly has been, more times than I care to think about, and only a few of those were the romantic kind. All sorts of things will break your heart, frankly; even joyful things, at times, can be heartbreaking. It is impossible to live without walking a great many dark trails along the way.

Many of the essays in this book, like much of my work over the years, reflect the darkest parts of the forest, the times when I came to a fork and didn't know which way to go, or when the brambles were overgrown and blocking the trail. That's a bit counter to the idea of optimism and cheer; it might seem as though I've plunked myself down in a hedge in the rain and refused to move, stuck indefinitely in the scratchy branches.

But writing has always helped me navigate. It's a kind of map-making, a way to figure out where I am, and why, and how. Reading does the same: I pick up details about other people's maps that add to my own, allowing for new shape or clarity. None of our maps are identical, but when we see a familiar path or a common landmark in each other's stories, it's comforting—and helpful. We realize, perhaps, that there are others just behind us, or just ahead, out of sight. We are not alone. I hope that you will see familiar paths here, common landmarks, a route that you once took or perhaps are walking along right now—and I hope that it will remind you that we're all travelling together, even if we can't see each other around the bends in the road.

We all have two lives, or so said Confucius. Our second life begins, he wrote, when we realize we only have one. Brené Brown wrote that midlife is when the universe leans in close and reminds you: stop wasting your time on things that don't matter.

My second life has begun in earnest now. Maybe yours has, too. The universe is whispering in our ears. It's time to figure out how we became the people we are, what we learned along the way about ourselves and the world, and who we might be in a future that is wildly unpredictable and uncertain. This book is my attempt to do just that: to map out where I've been, where I am right now, where I might be going. And I hope that you will see yourself here, travelling through this forest alongside me with only the moon to light our way. I'm grateful to have you here, happy for the company, and cheered—as I always have been—to know that I am not alone.

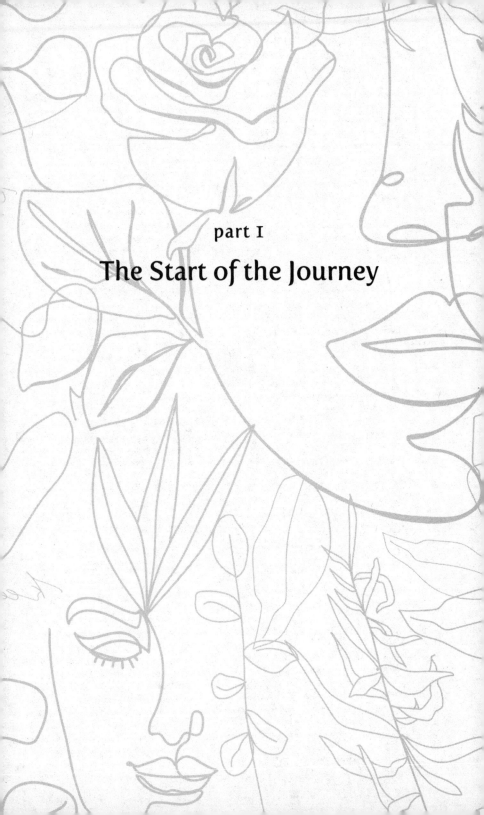

part I

The Start of the Journey

Rise and Fall and
Rise of the Bosom Friend

My first bosom friend was a little girl whose name I no longer remember, but we sat alongside each other on the bus to kindergarten every day. She was beautiful, small, and dainty, and she always wore pretty dresses with colourful tights. I was a little bit in love with her, in the way one understands love as a child: here is a person I would like to be with, all the time, forever.

Later there was Jamie, then Christine (whose mother was my mother's bosom friend as well, which was handy but doubly heartbreaking when we moved away), followed by an intense best-friendship with Alison, who was wild and gorgeous and had a waterbed and more freedom than any of the girls in our class. I smoked my first cigarette in her snowy backyard sometime in the sixth grade, and did a middling job of pretending I didn't want to wheeze up a lung while she was cool and collected, dropping the rest of her cigarette to the ground and crushing it under the toe of her boot, like a 1950s movie star.

There were other best friends in between, based less on personality and more on proximity—the best friend who always chose me first for dodgeball teams, the best friend on my street who went to a private Catholic school so we only saw each other on weekends, the best friend from summer day camp. The latter was short-lived and based on the most minor of factors: we were both late being picked up on the first day, and she liked my E.T. sneakers. At the age of seven, that was more than enough; we were attached at the hip for the two weeks of camp and then I never saw her again.

Later, in high school, there was a group of best friends whose lives were intricately interwoven with mine, and with each other. None of them was more or less important than the others. If I said that this one was my best friend on Monday, and then on Thursday I said it was another in the circle, I was honest each time: I needed them all, in different ways.

A single lifelong bosom friend—the kind that Anne Shirley had in Diana—was a luxury reserved for kids who grew up in one place. I moved with some regularity, transplanting multiple times, from British Columbia to Ontario, back to BC and then Ontario again, and on to Alberta before finally settling for good on the West Coast. I went to four elementary schools, followed by a junior high, a high school, then to a college in one city, a university in another, and finally a second university several hours away, all by the age of twenty-four.

By necessity, my bosom friends rotated in, and then out, of my life. But they were no less important to me than Diana was to Anne, or Anne to Diana. My mother has told me that my friends—even in the earliest years of elementary school, back to kindergarten, in fact—were the most important thing to me, the sun around which my life rotated. A falling-out could put me into a state for days, while a reconciliation would immediately right my ship again. I begged for sleepovers, where we could spend hours discussing all the very important things that needed sharing. The rest of the week, we'd simply talk on the phone for hours and hours (until a frustrated parent who had been waiting for a call would pick up another line somewhere else in the house and demand that we hang up).

My life hinged on my bosom friends, but it never occurred to me that theirs might hinge on me. I was the lucky one to be in their orbit, to be permitted to share in their worlds. That anyone might feel as lucky in reverse didn't enter my mind; it still doesn't today. They will be fine without me. I've always harboured a lingering fear that, one day, I'll have no friends at all.

Sometime in my thirties, this fear began to come true. I hadn't thought it would be possible, but my tight bonds with my female friends started to unravel. I would like to say that it wasn't my fault, but it often was, albeit in unintentional ways. It's easy to be available when you're young, when time is split between work and friends and not much else. Going out for a movie or dinner requires almost no planning. There's no one to check with, no babysitter to source. I could help friends move their couch, or I could sit on that couch and listen to them cry for hours after a breakup. I was accessible.

But my life didn't stay that way. People moved away for jobs or because they'd met someone who lived in another city. Schedules got busier and more demanding as careers grew. And over the span of a few years (which felt like overnight), I suddenly found myself with a husband, two small children, a house with a yard that needed mowing, and two cats. There were doctor's appointments, and volunteer duties at the school. Scout meetings to drive to. Work deadlines and long commutes. And there were hard things, too: aging parents, health issues, deaths in the family.

Life got busy. Very busy. I made new friends, most often with the other parents on the playground at school, or the writers I met when I returned to university to study writing. The old friends I saw the most often were the ones who lived nearby and had similarly aged children. For the most part, we had the same schedules, and no one minded when a dinner party ended at 7:30 p.m. so we could all go home to put the kids to bed. But even that got challenging as kids got older, our schedules filling up with softball games and piano lessons. Finding free time that overlaps between two families is like solving a Rubik's Cube. My social circle narrowed to a few close friends.

Social media had arrived and that helped, but no matter how much those platforms evolved and grew, it wasn't the same. I felt a persistent, vague guilt about losing touch with people, about not trying hard enough, about not being there for them—or, for that matter, not even knowing if they might need me to be there for them. Their lives were increasingly a mystery. Things looked great on social feeds, but what was going on behind the scenes? I had no idea. When we'd get together once or twice a year, I'd avoid personal topics, sticking to the safe stuff: How are your parents? How is work going? Any trips coming up?

I hated how superficial I sounded but I no longer had the day-to-day knowledge of their lives, and I wasn't sure I had the right to pry, as I once might have.

The downside and the upside to the extended circle of bosom friends, especially in high school, is that everyone has their role. And you get attached to that role, sometimes for good. Mine was being the keeper of secrets, the person to go to for advice. I was safe: I wasn't going to steal your boyfriend, and I didn't mind being the third wheel, which I was most of the time because my friends always had boyfriends and I did not. I was cautious, thoughtful. I had a good nose for trouble and avoiding it. I was the best at planning things. The organizer. Helpful. I was the funny one, the teller of tall tales and the memory bank.

Parents liked me because I talked to them about politics and gardens and said, "Thank you so much for having me," when I left.

A large part of the identity that I carried into adulthood was shaped around how people saw me in those years, for better or worse. I was proud that people confided in me, that they saw me as trustworthy. I was embarrassed that I was the third wheel and odd-girl-out, though I pretended not to notice. I liked that people thought I was smart, that I could make them laugh, that much older adults saw me (almost) as a peer. I hated that the boys we hung around with often forgot my name.

I've often wondered how I'd have fared through those years, and who I might have become, without my friends. Even now, just shy of fifty, I still think of myself with many of these descriptors. They are a comfort, and a limitation.

As much as others relied on me to be that person, it is fair to say I relied on them more. Friends were a safe place, a shield, protection. Your own personal army. When something bad happened to one of you, it happened to all of you. If a teacher was being a jerk to one friend, we all gave him the stink eye. If a popular girl was going after you, your friends had your back. If your period was late, your friends waited anxiously with you. If things were rough at home, you disappear to a friend's house. But friends were also laughter, and belonging, and goofing around and driving with the windows open and sneaking out to smoke cigarettes at the top of the waterfall in the park after midnight.

Friends were survival and joy, an antidote to loneliness, the cure-all for life.

I adore my alone time now. I can walk for hours in a big city, hike by myself on trails in the forest, disappear to a cabin for a few days of writing and solitude. I love going for dinner by myself, taking in a movie without company, or paddleboarding for a whole morning solo. I carve out my alone time from the rush of everyday life, and it is precious. When I come back home, after two hours or two days, I'm renewed and refreshed, the best version of myself.

But lately I'm finding myself with ever-larger pockets of alone time that I didn't create with intention. My kids have their own friends and interests and, more and more, their own lives. The busy days of driving them to Girl Guides meetings and the library and the pool are coming to an end. My career has changed, too. I work from home in a small office in my basement, with a tiny window that looks out on a patch of grass. Sometimes I smile and wave at the postal carrier, and sometimes, if I get lucky, they smile and wave back, the only person I might see for six or seven hours. Increasingly, I am not so much alone as I am lonely.

It turns out I enjoy my own company an awful lot, but only when it is optional.

I wonder now if perhaps I've never really learned to be alone without feeling lonely—except on those occasions when it's entirely by choice. When I was little, my three younger siblings were always around, a built-in playgroup.

As I got older, friends filled the gaps, then roommates and colleagues, and eventually my own children and husband. There has rarely been a time when I've been alone for long.

When I find myself in unfamiliar places where I don't know anyone—a new job, a conference, a classroom, a social event—I try to create a circle of familiar faces as quickly as possible, a group of short-term best friends to be my temporary safety net.

In recent years, this distinction between two different ways of being alone has become more obvious. The pandemic solidified and intensified a tiny handful of close friendships, but my wider circles drifted even further apart. Now I miss people. More specifically, I miss the no-secrets, share-everything, tight-knit closeness of those friendships earlier in my life, and the mutual reliance it permitted. Because I find myself needing that again, more than I ever expected to.

Midlife, it turns out, is a lot like puberty. I am lost in the same ways I was as a teenager: uncertain about my future, with a heap of weird stuff happening to my body, and a desperate need to know I am not alone in either of those things. Doing this solo makes it all harder than it ought to be. In midlife, the bosom friend must rise again.

When my father passed away more than a decade ago, I sent out word to my friends about the memorial gathering we were hosting at my parents' house. It was informal, low-key. Just some of his favourite foods, some wine. No service, no speeches. No big deal, I said, only if you're nearby. We had all gone to high school in this community but none of them, except one, still lived there. I was not expecting anyone to show.

But they did, en masse. My heart burst wide open. Maybe I had been present enough, after all, I thought. Maybe they knew that I meant well, that I was doing my best, that I was juggling every day.

A friend I had not seen in years arrived at the door, came up the stairs, and gave me a hug. I leaned into her and tried (and mostly failed) not to sob. Anyone watching would have assumed I was crying about my father, but it was her presence—what she knew about me, what she knew about my relationship with my father, what she knew about how messy and complicated this day would be for me—that caused the outburst. We had been like sisters once. I'd mourned our lost friendship for years, to the point I'd sought counselling to manage the overwhelming grief and guilt of it. It was harder than almost any romantic breakup that I'd experienced, and I've had a few doozies.

Such a thing sounds wild and foolish to anyone who hasn't experienced it. But I've heard other women talk of this: The loss of a bosom friend, at any age, can turn your world upside down. The love of a bosom friend can turn it right again.

I was a little bit healed that day, in a place I thought was too scarred over to repair. That's the miracle of friendship— a single drop has power.

...

These days, I think about starting a book club, or a walking group, or a coven. Want to meet me in the forest on the full moon? We can talk about hot flashes and drink tea and gather herbs and stuff. No? Okay, maybe a once-monthly brunch. Weekend getaways. Movie nights. Writers' meet-ups. I'd like to go dancing but I don't want to be up until two in the morning. We could do a pottery class together, and commiserate about raising teenagers and figure out what we're supposed to do with the rest of our lives while we make vases and mugs.

I'm up for anything, really. Because I don't think I'm the only one to notice this strange and unexpected blank space, like discovering an empty room in a house you've already lived in for years. We need our bosom friends. Still, again, always—not one or two, but several. We need our personal armies, our survival and joy. We need to talk, gossip, hug, laugh, cry. We need to tell someone how we feel and hear them say, "Oh my gosh, same here."

We need what we've always needed: to see ourselves in each other and to know, somehow, it's all going to be okay.

The Pencil Test

The first time I heard about the pencil test, I was sitting in a sea of sleeping bags and pillows, giddy on a combination of 7 Up and gossip. I was thirteen and midway through one of my first big sleepover parties. Our host, the queen bee of seventh grade, held up a pencil and explained the process.

"You put the pencil right under your boobs, like this," she said, pressing it close to her tank-top-covered rib cage, just below the swell of her small breasts. "Then you let go. If the pencil stays there, you have ... saggy ... boobs."

She let that sink in as we groaned and giggled, then she released the pencil, hands held high above her head. It fell to the ground, no saggy boob in sight to trap it. She grinned. "If it falls, you're okay."

Sleepovers are boot camp for girlhood, endless hours of talking about boys and kissing, painting toenails, and pretending to be older than you really are. We'd already played Truth or Dare, and made a prank phone call or two. We'd sat mesmerized, watching the newly released *Dirty Dancing*—the VHS tape and machine both rented specially for the occasion—then hashed over the plot, the characters, the clothes, the hair.

Just as we were beginning to settle down to sleep, Rosie (the birthday girl, whose mother was cool enough to rent *Dirty Dancing* and let us eat junk food all night) had stood up to tell us about the pencil test. It didn't occur to me to wonder where she'd gotten this information. She said it so authoritatively—one hip cocked to the side, eyebrow arched, confident grin—that it brooked no debate among the crew of girls.

I giggled and squealed along with the others, joined the chorus of "eww, gross!" mortified by the horror of imperfect breasts. I shrank into my Garfield nightshirt, keeping my own chest, without a doubt the biggest in the room, hidden as well as I could manage.

"Your turn," Rosie said, bending over to retrieve the pencil and handing it off to the girl nearest her.

That's when my panic set in. The pencil test wasn't just something we were going to talk about, it was something we were going to do. In front of each other. Doing what we girls do best as we enter adolescence: sizing up, ranking, judging, not so much to find fault in others but to figure out how much fault belongs to us, an accounting of all the ways we are wrong.

...

Two years earlier, the arrival of my period had been the harbinger of other changes, most notably my mother finally deciding it was far past the time for me to be wearing a support garment of some variety.

We think of airplanes passing overhead as loud. Chainsaws, too, or cars backfiring, or the sudden thunder of a summer rainstorm. None of these match, in volume, the sound of your own mother's voice in the Sears lingerie department asking the clerk for assistance to FIND A BRA FOR MY DAUGHTER!

She was probably whispering. My mother doesn't shout, and certainly not at store clerks. Nor was she dismissive of pubescent mortification or prone to making a public scene. But in that moment, her mild-mannered approach felt and sounded like the loudest and most public admission of unwanted cleavage in the history of the world.

I was so horrified by the entire proceedings that I've blocked the rest of the memory completely. I know this much: it was white, and there was a tiny pink rosebud between the cups, and when I got home it went directly into my drawer, where it stayed for a very long time.

In the logic of childhood, if it didn't exist, neither did my boobs. In truth, I needed that bra. My breasts weren't just starting to grow, they were already there. I hid them under big shirts, layers of sweaters with snug tank tops underneath, and learned to sit, walk, read, breathe, and live slightly curved over, shoulders hunched all day long, to minimize their appearance. I didn't know anyone else who had a box of Kotex in her backpack, or a white bra in their drawer. I refused to be the first.

By the time I was old enough to be sitting in that sea of sleeping bags and pillows, having breasts wasn't that big a deal anymore. Most girls had them, or at least the start of them—and retrospectively, I realize that the torture I felt over my big ones was the parallel torture of the girls who worried over their smaller ones.

But as we sat in that circle, and the pencil was being handed off to the next victim, I had no sympathy for the breastless or the barely there. I wanted to be them: lithe and slim, with bodies like Romanian gymnasts who scored perfect tens at the Olympics. As the pencil made its way around the circle, they wouldn't need to fear whether it would fall to their feet or stay trapped under a prematurely saggy breast.

As Rosie held the pencil out to that first girl, my heart thudded in my ears and my face burned red. I knew with total sinking certainty that I would fail the pencil test.

Are there any girls who came of age in the 1980s who didn't want to be Baby in *Dirty Dancing*? She was smart and funny, traits we still believed were important, traits we hadn't yet given up as being "dorky" or "unattractive." She was awkward and nervous; she didn't know how to kiss or dance or even how to do her hair properly, or match her shoes to her dress.

And Johnny. We might not have completely understood what sex was yet, but we knew Johnny was, somehow, sex—at least in a safe, soft sort of way. He was world-weary but kind, gentle but passionate, and Patrick Swayze was so goddamn good-looking that you wanted to die. We all wanted to be what he wanted: the girl who shows up in Keds, carrying a watermelon, a tangle of clumsy uncertainty, and unfolds like a flower into a desirable woman for whom you'd fight society just to dance with.

Even as I wished for it, I knew: I was no Baby.

Baby would have passed that pencil test with flying colours. Her huge-breasted sister, on the other hand, had a bosom that entered the room before she did. When she was made foolish and silly and ridiculous in all her bouncing and breastiness, when she was manhandled and mistreated, I don't think we felt any sympathy for her. What could someone expect, looking like that?

I managed to escape the pencil test that night. Thank goddess for the short attention spans of teenage girls. We moved on to something else, someone else, a new game, another story.

I left the party with that pencil in my head and it stayed there for thirty-some-odd years. As I got older, I made jokes about the pencil test, cackling over the various objects I might keep under my breasts. Just a pencil? Heck, why not the whole pencil case? Maybe a notebook? Box of Kleenex?

I laughed because it was easier than admitting that every time I took my shirt off, every time I tried on a bra, every time a partner saw me naked or I saw myself naked or I got undressed at the doctor's office, I thought of that sleepover and that pencil and the sinking horrible realization that I was not Baby, and never could be.

Decades later, half-heartedly listening to public radio as I wove through traffic on my commute home, I heard the words "pencil test." I turned up the volume, but I was too late, catching only the tail end of a discussion about women's bodies and self-image. When I got home, I googled "pencil test"—breath held, anxious to see if my childhood ghost indeed had a place in reality.

From Wikipedia: "A pencil is placed in the inframammary fold, between the breast and chest. If the pencil does not fall, the woman has 'failed the pencil test' and needs to wear a bra."

What? The woman needs to wear a bra? Not "the woman has awful breasts" or "the woman has failed in growing boobs that defy the laws of physics in their perkiness," but simply "needs to wear a bra"?

The pencil test, it turned out, had been devised by long-time advice columnist (and sister to Abby of Dear Abby fame) Ann Landers as a simple, though tacky (and no doubt scientifically inaccurate), measure of whether or not a young woman should start wearing a bra.

I followed the links at the end of the Wikipedia entry

and found more. In particular, this: "If the pencil stays put, then she is officially a woman, with all the attendant glories."

Attendant glories?

I wanted to cry, for not having known years ago—when I most needed to—that womanhood even came with attendant glories, that breasts that kept a pencil in place were no better or worse than those that didn't, that the test had been explained backwards. I was enraged that the test existed at all, and that it had crossed paths with my life at the worst possible point.

It was too late to go back and redo the first time I got to second base and hesitated, that damn pencil in my head; it was too late to buy the pretty bras instead of punishing myself with the ugly ones; it was too late to not wear turtlenecks for the majority of my twenties and thirties; it was too late to not apologize to the mammogram technician because she had to deal with my imperfect breasts.

How had I let something so foolish and insignificant define me for so long, so deeply? Somewhere inside me, my thirteen-year-old self, huddled in a Garfield nightie, desperate to escape that rec room, finally stood up, grabbed the pencil, and snapped it in half.

A Manual for Menstruation

How to perform the Tuck:
Reach into your locker. Be casual. Laugh with a friend
or pretend to watch something at the end of the hallway.
Fumble with the zipper on the front pocket of your backpack. There you go, slowly, slowly. Now slip your hand in
and grab your pad or tampon. Tuck it up into the sleeve
of your sweatshirt and grip the cuff tight in your fist, so
nothing slips out. (If you don't have long sleeves, swivel
your body so one hip is curved inside the locker, then tuck
the item into a back pocket or your waistband.) Step back
slightly, check the mirror hanging in your locker, grab the
textbook you need for the next class. Move slowly, like you
have all the time in the world, like this is any other day,
like you don't have mere minutes before there's going to
be a bloom of red on the seat of your pants because your
chemistry teacher wouldn't let you take a bathroom break

and you had to wait till this five-minute shuffle from one class to another. Just be cool, calm, collected. No one can know. No one can know you have your period, because, ugh, gross.

I was eleven when I got my period for the first time. It was springtime, a beautiful sunny day. I woke up to a houseful of out-of-town family and everyone preparing for a long drive to a wedding being held south of Edmonton, where we lived at the time. My mother had spent weeks sewing me a beautiful dress for the event: it featured a sweetheart neckline and pouf sleeves in a fabric of soft turquoise with lilac pinstripes. I had matching tights and shoes, both hand-me-downs that—by some cosmic magic—happened to be the exact right shade. The outfit was hanging over my chair, all the pieces laid out, waiting. I had gone to bed the night before thrilled and expectant, eager for the grown-up outfit awaiting me.

But when I woke up, I felt weird, overheated, achy. I dragged myself to the bathroom, sat down—and spent a solid ten seconds in frozen confusion staring down at my underpants. The dark stain was the colour of farm fields in Prince Edward Island, a muddy brown-red. Had I had an accident? Did I have the flu, some kind of tummy bug? Was I hurt and couldn't feel it? Was this cancer? Was I … dying?

Finally, it clicked: Ohhh, oh! This might be that. No. It couldn't be. But maybe? Is it? Could it be that?

That being the thing girls get between the ages of

twelve and sixteen, which lasts for five days each time, in a precise twenty-eight-day cycle. Or so I had been taught, in an awkward half-hour session earlier in the school year when they split the boys and girls into two rooms and my teacher, probably against her will but without any alternative, told us about bras and menstruation and pregnancy.

My mom had told me about it, too, but my primary memory of this conversation was that her mother, my grandmother, had never been told a single detail by anyone, including her own mother, which was a terrible thing to do to a young girl, so when it began, she really thought she was dying. It was important to know you weren't dying, and even though it might take you by surprise, it was totally normal. Apparently, that last part of the talk hadn't stuck, because I'd already considered the possibility that, yes, I could be dying.

My parents had also supplied us with several sex-ed books, which I had devoured with great interest. Unfortunately, I'd skipped over the pages on periods and pregnancy, and mostly focused on the in-between step. I was very, very curious about that in-between step.

As I sat there on the toilet, a sinking feeling in my stomach, all the evidence lining up in my head, I was increasingly sure this was *definitely* that, but what if? What if it wasn't? I was only eleven, and only by a couple months, and this was supposed to happen between twelve and sixteen. It was also the wrong colour entirely, not at all the colour of the blood that dripped from my knee when I skinned it. Maybe something was, in fact, very wrong with me. There was no alternative but to check with an expert. I waddled to the bathroom door and yelled in a voice that I hoped would express enough urgency to get my mother's attention, but not enough to draw anyone else's.

"Mom! Can you come up here, please?" My face burned red and hot. I could hear her footsteps on the stairs, the laughter of my aunts in the kitchen gossiping over morning coffee.

As I waited, sore and uncertain, I remembered the beautiful dress hanging in my room, maybe the most beautiful dress I had ever had and certainly the most grown-up outfit of my life to date. I burst into tears.

How to perform the Roll and Shuffle:
Wake up. Panic. You overslept and your pad is full. Full full full. Overfull. Throw back all the blankets. Pat your hand around the sheets under you. Still dry? Good. Scoot slowly to the edge of the bed, keeping your legs squeezed as tight as possible. Roll, like a log, off the side, so that both of your feet hit the ground at the same time. Stand, legs together. Ignore what gravity is doing to you now, and shuffle as fast as you can—but not too fast—to the nearest washroom. Shout at your little brother when he tries to come in.

Mom sorted me out fast enough, with a sanitary pad that looked about as big as the Danielle Steel novels I wasn't supposed to read, and another few spares for my purse that day. I walked back to my bedroom, bow-legged and awkward. I didn't want to talk to anyone, or do anything, or go anywhere. I wanted to lie in bed and cry. My eyes flicked to my bookshelf, to the spine of a Judy Blume book: the first book I'd read that talked about *all this*. Margaret never mentioned this part, I was sure of it. Everyone in that book was excited about getting their period, competitive even. Hadn't one of the girls lied about it to seem mature and cool? I thought I'd be excited about my period long before there was time for it to arrive, swapping notes with friends. I hadn't even talked to any of the girls in my class about the *idea* of periods, let alone actual ones. Our conversations were a mix of slightly more mature considerations, like if we'd be allowed to have a sleepover on the weekend and take the bus to West Edmonton Mall by ourselves, and childish ones, like whose Cabbage Patch doll was the prettiest (mine, obviously). The rest was supposed to be coming in junior high. Periods and bras and boys and dances and all that exciting stuff. But this wasn't exciting at all, only awful and uncomfortable.

I sat down on the floor and started pulling on the beautiful matching tights. Would they even fit with this … thing … in my underpants? I refused to cry again but I wanted to. I wanted to cry all day.

How to perform the Cover-Up:
Go to the washroom and discover you've got a problem. There's a big stain on your jeans, all the way through. If you

bend over at all, it will be visible. A scarlet letter where your thighs meet your bum. Everyone will know. Tidy yourself as much as possible. Change your pad. Pull up your pants. Wash your hands. Now, take off your sweater (this is why you wore a sweater in the first place, an emergency backup) and tie the arms around your middle, like it's a cape hanging from your waist. Grab some paper towel in case you left a mark on your desk seat. Make sure the paper towel is hidden; wad it up in your hand or in your pocket. Upon return, pretend to drop something next to your desk and check the seat. If you're all clear, grab the bottom hem of the sweater—casually, of course, don't want anyone to notice—to make sure it stays under you while you sit back down. Be uncomfortable. Be uncomfortable through the rest of the day and all the way home. But don't let on. You must always behave as though periods don't even exist.

A couple summers later, I spent two weeks at a distant cousin's farm. I didn't know her well but we were the same age, and another cousin was going to be there at the same time, too. My parents dropped me off, and within a few hours I was helping to collect the eggs, feed the goats, and brush the horses like I'd lived there my whole life. I loved it. We three girls slept in a small camper between the barn and the house, a first taste of independence. We stayed up late sitting around bonfires and woke up when the roosters began to crow.

One morning, my cousin's father saddled up three of

the gentlest horses and her mother packed a picnic lunch, and off we went for a trail ride. My period had started the night before, unexpected. In those first years, it was always unexpected, arriving three weeks late, one week early, appearing randomly with cycles that could be eighteen days or forty-three. There was no rhyme or reason to it, and certainly no way to plan for it, except to always be prepared.

It's hard to remember now just how big the pads were in the 1980s. Ultra-absorbent super-thin pads with wings hadn't been invented yet. What was available when I was thirteen was smaller than what my mother had used in the 1960s, but not by a lot (though thank goodness the belts had been replaced by adhesive strips long before I needed one).

Off I went on that gentle trail ride with a few spare pads in a backpack, plenty of optimism, and a sense of freedom. There was no teacher to get permission from to use the washroom, no boys around to see a stain on my pants. But I didn't know how to ride properly, the best way to sit in the saddle or when to use stirrups and when not to. We went up the hillside, down into the valley, and all the way to the creek where we were going to stop for a picnic, bouncing along in the heat, sweat dripping down my back.

It didn't take long for the pad to bunch up and move around and get very, very uncomfortable inside my denim jeans. I swapped it out after our break, taking care to wrap up the first one so I could bring it back home with me rather than discard it in the wilderness. Ten minutes into the return trip, the new one felt like a bulky wad of wet sports socks. I bounced and bounced and bounced all the way home, overheated in the late afternoon sun, and could barely walk by the time we returned.

I skipped dinner and lay in the camper. Eventually I told my cousin what was wrong, and she relayed it to her mother, who brought me into the house for a warm bath. When I emerged, she gave me a jar of skin cream, and instructions on where and how to use it, and then asked if I wanted her to teach me about tampons.

I spent the entirety of the next day lying on a blanket in the shade of a big oak tree, wearing an oversized T-shirt with cream on my "parts" to ease the friction rash, while my cousins played with the baby goats and went off to pick berries.

"This is bullshit. This is all such fucking bullshit," I thought to myself. Curse words were off limits, but I let myself think it anyway because, honestly, it *was* fucking bullshit. Boys never had to deal with any of this? Ever? They could go swimming or horse riding whenever they wanted? They didn't have to hide their pads in the sleeve of their sweater, or roll sideways out of bed in the morning to avoid a lava flow?

I still hadn't had a single excited conversation about periods. All of the expectation and excitement that I'd thought would be part of growing up just didn't exist. Periods sucked, and the rest of getting older didn't seem much better.

How to perform the Secret Agent:
In a public bathroom, open the packaging as slowly as possible. Don't make any noise. Better yet, wait for someone else to flush their toilet, then rip it open fast as possible so no one will hear. This is illogical; half the world's population gets a period. Whoever is in the stall next to you most likely has, has had, or will have a period and use pads or tampons that make noise when being opened. But don't question the logic. It will be *embarrassing* if you make a lot of noise. If you're staying over at a friend's house—or even worse, at a boyfriend's house—run the tap so no one can hear the *crinkle crinkle crinkle* of the paper backing. Fold everything up inside a dozen layers of tissue paper, and bury it as deeply in the garbage as possible.

Eventually it did become something to bond over, but not in a joyful way. This was collective complaint. My friends and I would groan over TV commercials that featured a smiling woman pouring blue liquid onto a length of white pad, and we'd make fun of the overly cheerful girls jumping on their beds in the tampon advertisements.

"I just get this overwhelming urge to have a pillow fight every time I get my period," I'd say. "And I just want to dance," someone would reply with a chuckle.

We could communicate an entire sentence with only a word and a look. If a friend pointed casually behind themselves, raised their eyebrows, and asked "Okay?" that meant: "Hey, I've got my period, am I clear or has anything come through?" If a friend pointed at your rear and whispered, "You've got something," you knew exactly what she meant. If necessary, a few friends could walk behind you, a flank of privacy, on your way to the bathroom.

Periods never did get exciting, but they did become what the preteen books had predicted: something that connected me to other women, a shared experience around which to find common ground, albeit one of general misery.

How to perform the Better Option:
After the internet is invented, find a blog talking about stuff you didn't know existed. Start googling. And google. And google. Discover there are other options. There are *better* options. Period cups, with cool names. Washable, reusable pads. Period underwear that looks like normal underwear. Discover that teenage girls are celebrating with period parties, complete with cake, and schools are lobbying to supply free products for students. Discover there are teenage boys on TikTok encouraging each other to carry menstrual products in their own backpacks for their friends and sisters. Ignore that you've been taught that your period is gross, a thing to hide and to suffer through each month, a curse that requires you to purchase costly products which create endless garbage every month. Your period is part of your life, for most of your life, and it's time to get acquainted. You're decades too late to hold your own period party with your friends, but it's never too late to celebrate by yourself.

...

The first time I use a menstrual cup, I'm certain I've lost it inside of me and will have to go to the hospital to have it surgically removed. I frantically watch YouTube videos describing insertion and removal. I reread the product pamphlet roughly 674 times. I bear down, as instructed. Nothing. It's gone. Has it floated somewhere near my lung, where it must now live forever? I know this is physically impossible, and yet ...

Finally, I figure it out. I repeat the process from scratch and it's easier this time. I do it again a third time, better still. I use it for a few hours on a day I don't have to leave the house, just in case, and it works perfectly. When I remove it, I pour out its contents into the toilet, watching the blood swirl into watery blooms. My eyes go wide in surprise; it's so beautiful, like this, red rose petals and cherry blossoms floating across a clear sky.

I want to tell someone, to write about it, but I'm not yet liberated enough to believe that talking about menstrual blood out loud, or writing about its beauty—in actual words on a piece of paper that a stranger might read—is an acceptable thing to do.

Standing over the toilet, I think about horse rides and cramps, stained bedsheets, missed pool days, and embarrassing accidents. I think about boys making jokes, teachers who won't let you use the washroom in the middle of class, about men asking if you're "on the rag" in a tone that is always torn between derision and ridicule.

As the blooms of red melt slowly together into soft pink, it does not feel like a curse, like something worthy of disgust, something shameful to hide. In those royal red blooms, for a brief moment, I have a glimpse that this was always something a little bit miraculous, something that should have been valued, as integral to my personhood as any other part of me, the truest calendar by which I will mark my entire life.

If You Could Just Change ... Everything

Click, click, click. The little yellow wheel has the numbers zero to twenty around the outside edge, marking off a day's worth of fat grams. It came with a booklet listing hundreds of foods and their associated fat content. Every time I eat something, I look up how many fat grams are in it—eleven grams in one egg, eight grams in a bran muffin, two grams in a low-fat yogourt—and move the dial the equivalent amount. All day long, my fingers rub against the wheel like it's a rosary in my pocket, clicking the total forward. It takes very little to hit the max. But if I stay under twenty grams a day, I'll lose weight. I've got all summer, eight long weeks. I could be thin by September, when school starts again.

Summer break is makeover season. Later, when my year is not organized around the school calendar, I'll be told that the months leading up to summer are in fact makeover season: if you begin in February or March, you'll have just enough time to get your body bikini-ready for beach season. It will also become any period of time leading up to a milestone event where photos are likely to be taken: a tropical vacation, your wedding, your high school reunion. Entire reality shows will be based around makeover seasons of varying lengths.

But as a teenager, makeovers are best tackled in the window of time between school letting out at the end of June and starting again right after Labour Day in September, so that you can go back to school a new, improved you.

These weeks are, of course, also for sleepovers, and working at your part-time job, and going to the carnival that sets up in the largest parking lot in town for a few days, and sneaking out to smoke with friends on the swing set in the playground at the local elementary school. But underneath it all is the imperative that, by the end of this, you should be thinner, prettier, with a better wardrobe and whiter teeth. Not just that you should be, but you could be, if you only work at it enough. This is your holy mission. And you'll have no one to blame but yourself if you don't manage it.

Wash, scrub, swipe. The face wash is foamy and smells astringent, and the scrub is a gritty mud made from the ground-up shells of nuts. It strips the top layers of my skin, which is something I just learned I'm supposed to do. It's *exfoliating*, a word I'd never heard before. The round white pads come out of the container drenched in a mysterious chemical solution that stings when it hits my face. But that's a good sign. It's ultra-deep cleaning. It's purifying. A baptism for zits, the sins of my skin. If I keep it up, my face will be clear by the time school starts in the fall.

The bible for this work is a stack of magazines: *YM*, *Seventeen*, *Teen*. Sometimes a *Cosmopolitan* or *Shape*, something meant for grown-up women but filled with models who are sixteen, seventeen, eighteen. They will be almost too old to fill these pages by the time they're actually women.

Every issue has its own set of commandments to be memorized and followed: eight ways to get his attention; ten tricks for better skin; three best bets for stronger abs. Look inside for a pull-out guide to your best school year yet! Look inside for a pull-out guide to your best prom yet! Look inside for your pull-out guide to a feel-good summer makeover! There's always a checklist or a pull-out guide— maps to navigate your improvement efforts.

There are also the diet books, the handouts from weight loss groups, the various programs and plans and pills that are sold on late-night TV, plus tidbits you'll pick up on daytime talk shows and from the older sisters of your friends. So many rules and tricks and tips and plans and goals, all aimed at changing you for the better.

This is the gospel of worthiness, and I've memorized

it chapter-and-verse: salvation is easy, if you could just change ... everything.

Spritz, spritz, spritz. Spray myself with Love's Baby Soft perfume to smell sweet. Spray myself with Hawaiian Tropic bronzing oil and lie in the sun. Spray my hair with Sun In to bleach it out to a Barbie-doll white-blond. I learn how to anoint myself: dab at the wrists and neck, at my pulse points. Spray into the air, and walk through the mist.

It's important to cover up the smell of my own body, the colour of my skin, the shade of my hair, though no one says that exactly. Instead, they say: You're great, of course, yes, fantastic! Celebrate yourself! You should be you, and no one else! But the text and the photos never quite line up. Look at all these better options, these better bodies. You still have choices: cheerful cheerleader, rebellious punk rocker, glamorous celebrity, cute class president. I look like none of them but I am assured that if I follow all the steps in the handy pull-out guide for a head-to-toe new-you-for-a-new-year, I might manage it.

When it's clear that the fat-gram clicker isn't working, I start fresh. There's always another option, another plan, another diet. This is the 1980s and early 1990s: every grocery store checkout line has a million magazines with makeovers on their covers and diets by the dozen. Cabbage soup diet. Cottage cheese diet. Canned tuna diet. Track your exchanges. Deal a meal. Most of them, though, are low-fat. However low your fat intake is, you can make it lower. Fat is definitely the problem, in your food and in your body. So you eat low-fat muffins. Low-fat pasta. Low-fat yogourt. Low-fat everything, so that you, too, can be low-fat.

I spend the whole summer before grade nine praying at the altar of Our Lady of Low Fat, and when September comes, I'm taller, my hips are curvier, and my boobs are bigger. I am enormous. Years later, I'll look at old photos and realize that I had the body of a full-grown woman when many of my classmates hadn't started developing yet. But in the moment, I have no perspective, no alternate message. I tower over most of the boys at school, who call me fat in various ways, with nicknames or jokes or hallway announcements—*wide load coming through, make room*. I join a weight loss group, and at the start of each meeting I stand up and recite a pledge that includes a phrase along the lines of "my excess weight is there for everyone to see how foolish I've been." This seems totally normal, good even, a public self-flagellation that echoes aloud what we already think about ourselves a thousand times a day.

Thirty years on, this oath will still echo in my head weekly, sometimes daily, the end conclusion to a hundred unsuccessful makeover seasons: *what a fool I have been, and everyone knows it.*

...

Buy, buy, buy. I spend every summer working: mowing lawns, cleaning houses, later selling burgers and ice cream cones at a water park, then eventually hawking beer and hot dogs to golfers. How much of the money disappears into fat-gram clickers and exfoliating face washes and body sprays? Before Instagram and influencers and click-to-buy, there were magazines and advertisements and going to the drugstore to shell out money to make yourself better. Makeover season isn't just something you do, it's something you purchase.

The final makeover season of high school is a flop. It's not limited to summer this time, but runs the entire senior year leading up to graduation, and I am certain I can be at least thinner, if not thin, by June. It doesn't happen. I fuss about how my arms look in my short-sleeved gown, a beautiful blue dress in crepe silk sewn by my mother. I stand in the back row of every group photo, or kneel down to make myself small. My stomach hurts by day's end from sucking it in for hours on end.

My faithful attendance to the commandments hasn't changed me in the slightest. It takes years to escape this church, a slow disentangling from the doctrine of the makeover. I wish I could say I don't participate at all but I still attend on special days, like a lapsed Catholic who takes in Christmas Eve services out of habit and guilt. A fashion magazine here, a podcast about self-improvement there, though I am half listening to the sermons now, lackadaisical in my attempts, rolling my eyes at the preachers from the back pew.

I'm not sure I'll ever silence the preaching entirely, its language too laid down in my brain to erase it permanently. Instead, I find a new prayer, and repeat it over and over and over: *There wasn't anything wrong with you in the first place.*

Me Too, Maybe?

I'm hired for my first real part-time job after an interview that lasts roughly four minutes, starting with the question of whether or not I have a boyfriend, and ending with instructions to return in two days for my training shift. I'll be working a cash register at a summertime concession stand, and the boss explains that everyone wears the same T-shirt, no exceptions, though you can choose your own bottoms.

"What size?" he asks.

Extra-large, please, I answer. I am praying there will be an extra-large among the turquoise blue shirts overflowing from the cardboard box at his elbow. I am only fifteen but I have a big bust, wide shoulders. I prefer clothing that's loose, that won't show my shape.

He digs through the pile, then hands me a shirt and turns away, already leaning back over his accounting ledger, making notes in it.

"Okay, thank you!" I say, enthusiastic, pleased to have been hired. It's minimum wage, $4.50 an hour, and I'm already adding up how much more I'll earn doing this than the housecleaning and babysitting that's kept my piggy bank full till now. "Thanks! See you Friday."

He waves a hand, and I've been dismissed. I don't check the T-shirt tag until I'm out in the parking lot. It's only a large. I hold it up to assess. Shit. Looks more like a medium. Maybe they didn't have anything bigger, I think. Maybe it was accidental. Later, I'll learn from the other staff that it doesn't matter what size you ask for, you'll be given a shirt at least one size smaller, to ensure it's tight-fitting. At least, that's how it works for the girls. The boys seem to be swallowed up in theirs.

We roll our eyes at this, but no one is shocked and certainly no one argues the point. It's not worth it.

That's how it is, when you're a girl. Perpetual navigation of what's worth it and what's not. Figuring out who is a risk, and who is not. Which men are truly safe, and which are creepy but won't follow through, and which ones seem normal at first glance, but aren't. There are harmless teachers, and dicey ones. Dads who drive you home from babysitting jobs and barely blink, let alone dare to talk, and other ones who ask about your boyfriend and tell you how mature you are. Older boys in your school who are shy and nervous, and wouldn't touch you if you invited them to, and others who think it's hilarious to slide their fingers between your thighs when you're climbing the stairs ahead of them, so you'll jump and yelp.

On the scale of bosses, one that hands you a too-small shirt is pretty minor, something we laugh about behind his back. There are worse bosses to come.

We have no words for this. If someone said predator, we'd think of a lion. Toxic? Like acid rain, we'd have asked? Coercive control—is that a thing that spies do while interrogating bad guys? The #MeToo movement is decades away, and we're growing up in an era where we are told to fear the rapists who jump out of bushes, the kidnappers who lure children with promises of candy, and wife beaters. (Though this last category has some wiggle room, like what did she *do* to make him so mad? She must have done *something*, right?)

Everything else is just how the world works, and the responsibility is on us to avoid, ameliorate, appease. It is our job to absorb it. Men will catcall you, but aren't you flattered by it? Groups of guys in cars will slow down to ask if you want a ride, and you have to find a way to say *no* that won't make them mad—but they're just being nice, aren't they? Boyfriends are almost always several years older than their girlfriends, even if the girlfriends are still in high school, and no one thinks this at all odd since girls obviously mature much faster than boys, right?

By the time I'm seventeen, I've had my rear end patted by much-older male co-workers, two teachers, a friend's father, a tennis instructor, and at least three of my friends' boyfriends. A spontaneous game broke out in the kitchen

I was working in, one Saturday night, in which the all-male staff took turns guessing my bra size. One offered to check, googly eyed, his hands reaching out towards me like a lusty zombie. Everyone laughed. I laughed, too, because what else can you do? Customers make lewd jokes, ask about my age, tell me how mature I am compared to other girls. I've been cornered in empty rooms, pinned to the ground by someone bigger and stronger than me, stuck in a car with someone who threatened a "good time," always escaping by one part instinct and nine parts luck.

But all this is nothing, in the tally of what counts and what doesn't. I'm one of the lucky ones. I know this to the core of my not-yet-fully-grown bones. I've got friends who've been hurt in terrible ways, as children, as young women. Friends who don't mean to make their boyfriends so mad but they do, until he can't help but shove her, grab her wrist. Friends who have done things they didn't want to do, with men they couldn't get away from. Friends who are not safe at home, or at school, or at jobs.

I am late to dating, compared to my peers. Unless you count the boyfriend in grade eight, who waited for me at the bike racks, and asked if he could have one of my school photos which had just been handed out. I agreed, and somehow that meant, in the universal code of junior high, that we were now an item. A very, very innocent item. We held hands, and went to the movies, and he showed me his hockey cards. But that was it. Later, another girl who was interested in him asked me if he was a good kisser, and I lied: yeah, so great, the best. But I had no idea. We'd never kissed even once.

It's a long time before anyone holds my hand again. I pine through one teenage crush after another, unsuccessfully. I'm chubby, the dork of my group, a cheerful third wheel. I hate being the single one, but I'm mostly terrified by boys and men anyway: the younger ones bully and tease and pull out chairs a split second before you're going to sit down in them; the older ones are bold and crude, or touch you in sneaky ways you can't quite describe as wrong. It will be years before I understand that watching from the sidelines is far safer for my heart, and my body, than actually getting the guy.

I am eighteen, in the final months of my last year of high school, when I have my first serious romance, and it is followed a couple years later with another one, then another shortly after I leave university. In each case, there's a significant age gap: we are eighteen and twenty-four in the first one, twenty and twenty-eight in the second, and then twenty-six and fifty in the third. They are all far more sexually experienced than I am. In two, we work together; in both cases, I am the junior employee.

They all end badly, because that's how most things end. It is maybe better to say they all end with a broken heart, mine or theirs but not both (because that's also how most things end, isn't it, with one person ready to say farewell and one not).

But before these relationships end, they are wonderful:

these are fun, intelligent, engaging partners who are open-minded, progressive men with sex-positive and body-positive attitudes, descriptors I can only apply looking back—those terms may have existed in the mid-1990s but I didn't have the lexicon yet. I don't feel pressured or manipulated. Never cornered or bullied. I am not prey; it is mutual pursuit, initiated by me.

Rather than tearing me down, as so many early romances seem to, I leave these relationships with a sense of agency, of choosing for myself, of being in control. Each of them propels me further into adulthood and into my own sense of self, and of independence. It isn't until I describe this to friends in the future who look at me with blank expressions that I realize how unusual this is.

See? I said I was lucky.

When #MeToo comes, it comes at first for the most egregious, the most clear-cut, the most obvious: the serial predators, the abusers, the rapists, the frat boys who drop powders into beer bottles, the husbands who shove wives against walls, the wealthy who can manipulate their way out of any accusation.

Then it comes for the boyfriends who guilt their girlfriends into sex, for the street harassment and catcalling, for the handsy teachers, and the bosses who corner girls in copy rooms and walk-in coolers.

And oh, how we celebrate. Naming these acts out loud in a public forum, rather than around a kitchen table in whispers, is like watching an empire collapse and a new one being built from the ashes. It couldn't have been more aptly named: Yes, that happened to me. You, too? And you as well? Yes, and to me. It happened to me, too. We are united over our common experiences. We're not strangers anymore, we're humans with shared stories that are being told out loud, without shame.

Some men seem genuinely shocked by it all, others don't want to meet your eyes. Still others will tell you this has gone too far, no one can even smile at a woman anymore without getting in trouble. As I think back on too-small T-shirts and guessing games about my bra size, I wonder how many men are also thinking back to their own earlier interactions, re-evaluating them. Are they worried?

As the conversations deepen, it slowly expands to include all the many ways that harassment and sexism can happen: jokes around boardroom tables, inappropriate touches while working late on a project, age gaps and power gaps.

Scrolling the #MeToo hashtag late one night on social media, I come across a tweet about teenage girls—sixteen, seventeen, eighteen—dating young men in their twenties. How they convince themselves, for years even, that these are empowering experiences in which they were in complete control, treated as an equal adult partner in a consenting relationship. And that a large age gap with, say, a woman in her midtwenties and a man in his fifties, creates a power dynamic that favours the man. Always. I don't remember the exact words, but the message is like a bullet: even if you felt mature, you weren't mature enough to make that decision; even if you believed there was no power imbalance, there was.

It's the first time it occurs to me that relationships I had viewed as affirming and powerful might not have been.

Sifting through memories is, at the best of times, a heartbreaking experience: reliving awful events or joyful moments can both feel like a kind of grief. The former sparks regret, a wish to do over; the latter is a reminder of a time that is gone and won't return.

I still feel like I was one of the lucky ones, that I avoided being hurt or worse, in a world that was not safe for girls and women. But I also realize that all those things I summed up as no big deal—the comments and catcalls, the inappropriate touches and jokes—were in fact a big deal; they shaped how safe, or unsafe, I would feel in my body for my entire life.

But wrestling with the notion that these early romantic relationships were damaging and toxic—when they felt (and still feel) positive—has been challenging. When I take myself and the individual men out of the equation and consider the question of each relationship by impersonal details—ages, experience, the balance of power—as though I am evaluating the story of strangers, I know exactly how I would respond from the vantage point of another thirty years of life: that young woman has no idea what she's doing.

But I can't separate myself from the story: who I was, my life to that point, what I knew about my own needs and wants, the certainty of my desire, the degree to which my voice was heard by the men with whom I shared myself. And all of that tells me that I knew exactly what I was doing, and more importantly, that I wouldn't undo any of it.

So I'm left floating between these uncertainties: me, too, maybe—or maybe not. One answer will allow me to keep a story about my life that has been powerful and validating, while the other will require that I consider a different version altogether, one that casts me into a role I don't want for myself, or for the men I cared deeply about.

Like so many things, it's a question that will never be fully answered; it will echo through the coming years and colour how I worry about my children as they now approach adulthood themselves.

The world has changed a lot, but not enough for me to have any certainty that they will be safe. Even after all this progress, after naming the problem, after the revolution and riot, it doesn't seem so impossible to imagine my daughter being handed a uniform shirt that is two sizes too small.

The Witch in the Closet

It began, as so many wonderful things do, in the pages of a book. Specifically, one that I probably wasn't supposed to be reading at thirteen, tucked away in the darkened back corners of the local library.

This book was dark blue, with silvery grey writing on the front and an image of a large tree, with curlicues for branches and long twisting roots. I've tried to find it again, guessing at possible titles, googling cover images, hoping one will be familiar. But no luck: I read it just the once, dropped it off at the library a week later, and have never seen it since.

But I remember what it said, the heart of its message: Women are powerful. Women, in fact, *have* power. We've just been tricked into forgetting it.

. . .

I suppose it actually began years earlier, the seed of it anyway, sitting at my granny's kitchen table. She was, by any measurement, an odd duck. She made tea by brewing it in a pot on the stove—not with tea bags, like normal grandmothers, but with bits of bark, dried leaves, and berries. Her windowsill was full of glass jars, each containing items both mysterious and familiar: dandelion heads, withered roots, dried mushrooms, powders in all sorts of colours. None were labelled. She knew what each one was by glancing at it.

Of all my siblings, I spent the most time with Granny, because I was the oldest. During visits, I'd often stay over at her house, while the other children and my parents stayed with friends or family. I loved being singled out, but also dreaded being far away from my own mother. It was like a day at the carnival: hard to predict what wild thing might happen next and whether the ride would be fun or scary. It was a treat to go, but a relief to return home when it was all over.

She could be loud, embarrassingly so at times, dressed in gumboots and denim coveralls and less aware of social graces, it seemed, than I was even as a child. Depending on the day, she could also be erratic, even manic, dropping into episodes of heavy prayer that lasted for fifteen or twenty minutes, like she had forgotten I was there. Jesus, she often claimed, spoke to her directly—but so did various ancestors, ancient gods, the spirits of particular animals, the trees themselves, and more. She might decide on the spur of the moment we were going to go swim in the ocean in February, making a pit stop along the way at the Sally Ann thrift to find a second-hand swimsuit for me, never thinking it was strange to insist I wear it without washing it first, or that I might not want to change in the backseat of a car. Other times, she'd bring me along to meet up with friends, all of them at least as odd if not more, or we'd go off to flea markets and dusty used bookshops, or into Chinatown to get various medicines out of big glass jars.

The thing I liked best was when we went tromping through the woods, with no one else around. She'd march ahead, calling out cheerful hellos to the trees and bushes, her enormous brown-black husky, Jake, bounding between us. She'd show me the pink flowers of the salmonberries, the wispy moss that dangled off the tree branches, the furry gills on the underside of mushrooms. Later, back at the house with mugs full of mystery brew, she'd pull out big scraps of paper and have me draw what we'd seen, then colour and label them.

During one of our forest walks, she paused in a sunny clearing, pulled a little spade out of her pocket, and kneeled down, pushing the sharp edge of the metal deep under a small plant, far enough down to capture all the roots. She took a bread bag out of her pocket, shook it out to open the top, then tucked the plant inside to take home. I turned to go, but she called me back, still kneeling.

"We say thank you," she said, putting her hand down flat into the miniature crater that was left behind in the plant's absence.

She always talked to plants and animals, and even to

rocks and water, as though they could understand her. The world still existed for me in a binary: there were people, and then everything else. Animals might respond, but trees? The creek? The dirt underfoot? I felt foolish when I tried.

"Thank you," I whispered, a meek and uncertain sound. She nodded, closed her eyes, whispered something, and then stood. Later, while I ate dinner at the small kitchen table, she shook the plant over the sink to get rid of the dry dirt, then strung it up in the pantry, where it hung alongside other plants.

"What's it for?" I asked.

For your liver, she told me. I don't think I knew what a liver was, exactly, but I knew she meant medicine, something to *help* your liver.

She picked up a small silver tea ball, letting it dangle from the chain between two fingers, and spun it close by her ear. This was one of the ways she received messages from Jesus. She closed her eyes and began a monotone hum.

I didn't like watching when she did this, and looked away, attending to my drawings. I wasn't so sure about Jesus chatting through a tea strainer. But I liked the idea that powerful things came through plants, and that you could harness them, if you learned their language and knew them well enough.

Nature, too, had power. And it was willing to share it with us. Another thing we'd been taught to forget.

...

Perhaps that's how I ended up with that blue book in my hand. By the time I was a teenager, Granny had died and my memories of her were therefore finite and already becoming blurry with the passage of time. But I knew two things for sure: first, that she had likely suffered with more than one unnamed (but not unfamiliar in the family line) mental health challenge, no doubt exacerbated by behaving in ways a woman was not supposed to for most of her life; and second, she knew an awful lot, information I'd be unlikely to find in a book, most of which I did not remember but wished I could.

This legacy was its own kind of gift: yes, you might seem odd, but that didn't mean you couldn't know true things. Marching around the woods with her had given me the notion that there was mystery in the world, if you knew where to look—and it was most definitely worth going to look.

In a pre-internet world, in a small town that was almost exclusively white and Protestant, mystery was hard to come by, even if you were looking for it. Hence my habit of trawling through the non-fiction section of the local library to see what I might catch in my net. I had more or less memorized the categories and their order along the Dewey Decimal System. Philosophy, religions, psychology, natural science, history, geography. They all had something to say about people, in one way or another, and people fascinated me. What were their lives like? How did they dress and dance and celebrate? What did they believe about creation and the afterlife? And what could their lives tell me about my own?

It was the intersection of the natural world and the spiritual one that most captured me. For a while this dipped into the realm of fantasy, the weird books that hid in the margins between those Dewey categories. Sasquatch and aliens lived at the edge of the biology or astronomy sections. Atlantis and the Bermuda Triangle could be found between history and geography. Not quite philosophy, nor religion, were all the books about the unknown power the universe might or might not hold in the form of ancient religions, psychic abilities, spirits, ghosts. There was an endless supply of mystery to be found here: Stonehenge and crop circles and alien abductions and spontaneous combustion. Exorcisms. Frogs falling from the sky. Weeping religious statues. The Loch Ness monster. I loved reading these books, always with serious skepticism but also with the frequent refrain of "but, what if?"

It wasn't a question I asked out loud. That would be foolish, revealing a lack of rational thinking and education, a risk I knew as well then as I do today. But "what if" was a question that left room for possibility and for humility: to recognize that there could be, and most likely were, mysteries beyond what we can see or understand.

When I picked up that blue book with the silver writing, I was familiar with the historical idea of witches—women who had been falsely accused of all manner of sins, simply to control them, accuse them, and ultimately to kill them. I knew about Salem, and the European witch purges, and the misogyny that underlined the hysteria on both sides of the Atlantic. I knew too about the Hollywood version of witchcraft, the sort that came with twitching noses and black cats, or striped socks and sparkly red shoes sticking out from under a house.

But I wasn't familiar with the idea that a witch could mean something else entirely: a wise woman who had knowledge about the natural world, and that this knowledge—not a cauldron full of newt eyes—conferred power.

Why had this been deemed supernatural, or worse, a sign of the devil himself? It was only being aware of the miracles that already existed in every forest, field, river, in the patterns of the moon, the tides, the seasons, miracles which a woman might have been taught by her own mother or grandmother, or which she sought out and taught herself.

Framed like this, it was easy to imagine a time when being a woman, being a little bit magical, was not something to land you in a noose, but something sacred—a word I had never once associated with being a woman.

I was barely twenty when I saw *The Craft* a few weeks after it was released. It had the kind of witchcraft that was built on Hollywood special effects and myth, complete with summoning circles and spells and chanting. People levitated. Candles flickered to life with a single glance. Silly but seductive, especially on the big screen.

The film features a trio of would-be teenage witches who suddenly develop genuine magical powers when a fourth girl—a true-born witch, it turns out—joins their informal coven. Teenage girls and young women in the audience could see themselves in these characters: outcasts, weirdos, uncertain and awkward. They don't fit in, like so many of us, and are subject to the whims of authority figures, mean girls, and men who are predators. Their new-found magic makes them powerful, not just in spell-casting but in other ways, too: socially, romantically, financially. The potential love interest spreads rumours about one of the girls, then forces himself on another; his punishment is death, helped along with a magic spell. Obviously, murder (regardless of the motive) was going too far. The main character doesn't condone the act, but my hunch is that most of the young women in the audience felt some celebration in the moment, a theatrical imaginary revenge for the kind of harm already perpetrated against many of us in the real world.

In an era of movies about nerdy girls getting makeovers so they could date the popular guy, and choreographed dance routines spontaneously breaking out at high school proms, watching *The Craft* felt a little bit revolutionary. Here were young women whose power was not diminished by being female, but enhanced by it. They tapped into a Hollywood version of that inherited knowledge which already existed in each of them to varying degrees, but was magnified and made real by their connection to each other.

A heady notion. Girls, you aren't weak at all. You never were. You have something special inside of you and it's made stronger in the company of other women, in the collective, by coming together.

...

I've long been convinced that most women, at some point during their teens or twenties, go through a witch phase. It starts with a book, like the one I found in the library that day. Or a deck of tarot cards or a pretty crystal or a pack of charm candles in a rainbow of colours. It might begin with being struck by the beauty of the full moon on a dark night, or discovering that those dandelions in the yard will make good medicine or wine, depending on what you do with them.

I'm equally convinced that they mostly keep quiet about it, knowing they'll be open to derision. Men will snicker. Other women will, too. They'll appear irrational or illogical, or be deemed anti-science and uneducated. In some religious circles, they'd still be considered dangerous heathens suffering from the possession of demons.

So they carry on quietly, making note of the passing seasons—marking the solstices and equinoxes—and the moon cycles, and learning which herbs will treat which ailments. They don't talk about it much, or only with the right people. It gives them comfort, this awareness and attendance to the cycles of life, to the natural world around them, to the connection with others.

It reminds them that men have not always been in charge, that once upon a time the knowledge that women held—of the natural world, of the spirituality to be found in all that exists around us—was sacred, and that in other women they might find a collective kind of power, one that seeks to improve the world, not tear it apart.

...

My inner witch has been in the closet since the day I pulled that book from the shelf in the library, and traced my fingers over the silvery tree branches on its cover. But every year, she gets a bit louder, a bit bolder. She finds more of her own coven, which is just a fancy way of saying like-minded and gentle-hearted women. She doesn't mind so much that the things she knows with logic are sometimes a little bit different than the things she knows with instinct. There's room for both, now. She's old enough to not worry about who might burn her at the metaphorical stake, smart enough to realize there's far more in this world that she doesn't know yet than what she does. And she's too busy looking at the full moon and filling up jars with dried berries, revelling in the miracles that exist in the forests and fields, in the tides and the seasons.

She's learning that wise women, it turns out, begin as curious girls.

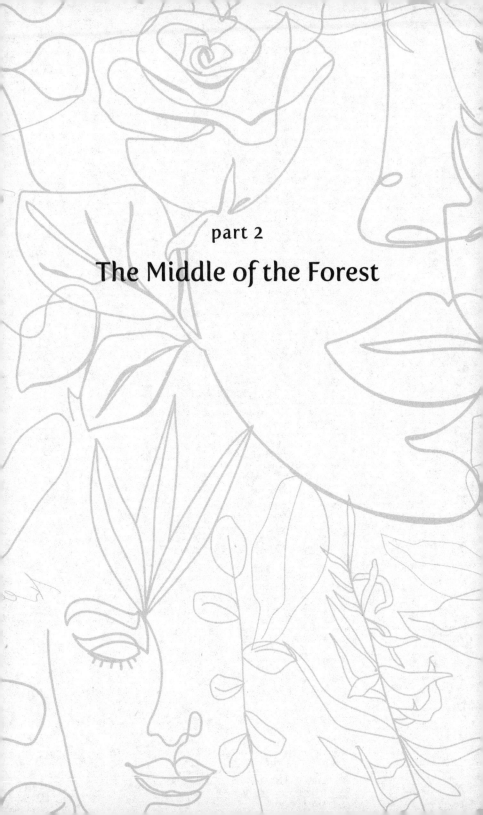

part 2

The Middle of the Forest

This Necessary Amnesia

"I don't think I can go to school today."

My daughter's voice is hoarse, and she opens her eyes for a second, squinting against the glare of the morning light. I can tell by looking at her that she's not well: her cheeks are pink and flushed, and her eyes are a little glassy. She's had a mild cough all weekend. I'd already planned to keep her home from school today.

But I go through the motions anyway, assessing her condition. I sit on the edge of the bed and lean over to press the palm of my hand to her forehead. I pretend that I am thinking, pondering, considering. Then I pretend that her hair is in the way, and start over so I can press my hand to her forehead a second time, leaving it there for five seconds, then ten, fifteen.

I can feel the warmth of her body against my leg, the soft skin of her face under my palm. I linger as long as possible, dragging it out.

I want to stay, to climb under the blanket and listen to her breathing, murmur *Mommy is here* and *everything is okay now*, as I have so many times before. I want her to hear my voice and tuck her head into my shoulder, seeking comfort in a place she knows she will find it. But I can't, and she won't. She's too old for all that now. There will be no cuddles, no taking care; she won't want me to stay nearby as she rests.

So I tell her I'll go get the thermometer, I'll refill the humidifier, and I'll get some Tylenol (the adult stuff now, no more grape-flavoured liquid in this house). I tell her to hold tight, that I'll be back soon. She nods, shifts her body away from me so that her hip is no longer pressed against my leg, and burrows down into her blanket, head disappearing entirely.

"Can you turn the light off?" she asks, a statement more than a question.

I've been dismissed.

"Of course." My throat closes around the word, tears pricking at my eyes.

I shut off the light, close the door, and retreat.

Once upon a time, it was hard to tell where I ended and my children began. Before they were born, of course, we were literally one—their survival dependent on my own for nine long months. My food was their food, my blood their blood. As they grew, I grew, too. Every kick and hiccup and roll echoed across my belly in ripples and bumps.

But even after they were born, the line between us remained blurry, sometimes invisible, melting in the intensity of those early years of mothering.

I carried both of them in baby slings at first, then baby wraps, and later in steel-framed backpack carriers for long walks on dirt trails. I took showers while they lay in bouncy chairs on the bathroom floor, peeking out the curtain every few seconds to smile and play peekaboo. I brought them into the bath with me, washed their little bodies first, then my own. I took eighteen months off after my first was born, twelve when my second was born, and then left my job entirely just before they turned six and three. I was with them all day, every day. We went to the pool, the park, the library.

My first-born always wanted "up, up, up," which was his way of asking to sit on my lap for a cuddle and be as close to me as possible. At tot drop-ins and play dates, he'd race off to jump and climb and kick the ball, but every few minutes he'd return for an "up, up, up" interlude. In one of the few videos I have from his early childhood, he interrupts himself mid-thought to ask "Up?" I encourage him to continue sharing his story, but a moment later, he asks again: "Up?" The camera wobbles, then the recording ends. I had to set it down so I could help him climb up.

He says now that one of his first memories is of asking to get up on my lap, but I was very pregnant and told him there wasn't really room anymore. I was probably also nauseous; I had morning sickness twenty-four hours a day for most of both pregnancies. I am not surprised I said no, but I hate to think that of all the times he ever asked to get up, the one he remembers is the time I declined.

My second was not so much an "up, up, up" child. But she was a cuddler, particularly a midnight cuddler. She'd appear, bedside, in the middle of the night. "Get in?" she'd say, more a statement than a question (a pattern, apparently).

I'd lift the blankets and she'd crawl in, lie down, and tuck herself into the curved space of my body. When she was little, I'd wait until she had dozed off, then move her back to her own bed, knowing we would all get a better sleep that way. But I never said no to the request.

People often told me that letting kids into your bed in the middle of the night was a bad idea. They'd get used to it, not be able to sleep without you, have a hard time self-soothing when necessary. My answer was always the same: I've never heard of a teenager that still wants, or needs, to sleep with a parent.

I knew it would drift away as she got older, and inevitably it did. When she was about eleven, the requests to "get in" became less frequent. No matter how tired I was, how much I could have used the uninterrupted sleep, no matter how much room her growing body took up in the bed, I still never said no. Eventually she would ask for the last time and I didn't want to miss it.

Months passed without a single middle-of-the-night appearance. I figured that was it, the final night had passed, unmarked. Then, a few months after her twelfth birthday, while my husband was away on a fishing trip, she arrived like a zombie, eyes closed, and asked to get in. "Of course, of course," I said, and flung back the blankets, letting her take the warm spot while I shuffled over to the empty cold side. After she fell asleep, she rolled into me, her head pressed against my arm, her slow breath tickling my skin.

I thought to myself: "This is it, for sure. This is the last time. Remember this. Remember this." I fell asleep wishing I could have another night and another night, but knowing I would not.

At some point, she must have wandered back to her own room; she was asleep in her bed when I woke up in the morning, and later when I asked about her midnight arrival—*Did you have a bad dream, was your room cold?*—she didn't recall having woken up at all or being in my room.

Like so many mothering memories, this final night of sleeping alongside my child is something that only one of us will remember.

They are teenagers now. Bedroom doors are closed, bathroom doors are locked. It's hard to recall the mindless ease of slipping in and out of bedrooms while they dressed for the day, or sitting by the side of the bath while someone made bubbles. I wouldn't dare to mention that, once upon a time, we took baths together, or slept cuddled up. They'd cringe. Or worse, they'd call *me* "cringe," which is the modern-day version of "you're so embarrassing, Mom."

But I think of these things often, when they laugh a particular way and I see their toddler faces still hiding there in the lines of their almost-grown-up faces, or when they're upset and stressed, and by instinct my hands move to hug, to rub a shoulder, to comfort. I think of it when we go for walks—increasingly less frequent—and I still reach, unthinking, for their not-so-little hands when we have to cross a busy street.

I think, too, of how many days I spent with barely a single minute untouched by another human being, how I couldn't pee alone or change alone or go to sleep alone or shop alone or shower alone. I think of how often I wished desperately to be alone for a few minutes, to have some solitary time with my own body and my own thoughts. How going to the dentist felt like a trip to the spa, because for an hour or so, no one needed me for anything, other than to lie down in silence. I resented, as most parents do, the wistful admonition by older parents to enjoy it while it lasts. It was hard then, nearly impossible in fact, to imagine that I might wish for more of the intensity of early parenting, to wish not to be alone, waiting for someone to ask me to go for a walk, to tell me some secrets, to cozy up on the couch and watch *Frosty the Snowman* for the hundredth time on a well-worn DVD. But here I am, wishing and waiting.

To be a mother, it seems, is to be forever in the process of remembering and forgetting, tucking away small memories and erasing others. It is coming to the end of the day and recalling only the times you messed up—when you were short-tempered, or frustrated, when you didn't spend long enough down on the floor playing with trains or you fed your child fast food in the car because you were late for an appointment. It's also, paradoxically, looking back from the distance of a few years and somehow forgetting all the hard things and rewatching everything through a golden haze: gone is the colic and the sleepless nights and the hundreds of pieces of Lego that bit into your foot while walking through the living room. All that remains of the past is the soft fuzz of a baby's head, or the way a child looked fast asleep with their little bum in the air and their tiny toddler arms tucked underneath them, or how they whispered all their secrets to you from morning to night.

We remember the best days, the loudest giggles, the tightest hugs. And then, too, we remember the days that fill us with regret, the days we wish we could redo with more patience and love and calm. Both are a kind of torture: here, remember this beautiful thing you no longer have ... here, remember this awful thing you wish you could change. And the brain runs over and through and around both of these, as though replaying the memories often enough might somehow change them.

Parenting is the only job that I know of in which one's goal is to make yourself functionally obsolete over time. It is to invest every part of yourself in something that will, that must, one day leave you. And, along the way, to force yourself into this necessary amnesia of forgetting what it was like when there was no line between you, because remembering is to ache with longing.

There is no alternative to it. I'd simply assumed I was better prepared for the transition.

Your children are not your children.
They are the sons and daughters of Life's longing for itself.

I recite these lines over and over, a passage from Kahlil Gibran's poem "On Children," while I fold laundry or wash dishes or walk alone in the deep ravine near my house. It is one of the truest things about being a mother I have ever read. It continues:

They come through you but not from you,
And though they are with you yet they belong not to you.

You may give them your love but not your thoughts,
For they have their own thoughts.
You may house their bodies but not their souls,
For their souls dwell in the house of tomorrow, which you cannot visit, not even in your dreams.

These are not my children now. They never really belonged to me at all. They belong only to themselves, as they always have, and to a future where I will not exist, someday. The house of tomorrow waits for them alone.

...

During a recent visit from some out-of-town friends, my son's bedroom was turned into a temporary spare room for guests. He slept the first night in the basement, the second on the couch, and the third night he fell asleep—while the rest of us watched a movie—on my bed, fully dressed. He's too big to move, and rousing him from deep sleep seemed cruel. My husband volunteered to take the couch and went back downstairs; I grabbed a second blanket (the first had been wrapped entirely around my son's body like a cocoon) and fell asleep next to him.

Sometime after midnight, I woke with a jolt—there was a muffled noise, talking, twisting. He was having a bad dream.

"Hey bud, it's okay. Shhhh," I whispered. "You're just having a nightmare, it's okay, it's okay. You're okay. I'm right here."

He must have heard me because the rustling stopped. He reached his hand out.

"Mum? Mum." He was mumbling, still in a foggy state of dreams and half-sleep.

"I'm here." I touched his hand. "I'm here."

He gripped it, hard. "Love you," he said, then snored. His hand—so much larger than my own now—held tight. I fell asleep rubbing my thumb across the back of his hand.

The line between us is more defined with each passing year, a border that becomes wider and more permanent every day. But once in a while, still, the line is thin. Once in a while, we are still like one.

Heart Attack Club

Heart Attack Club is me and seven guys. It's like Snow White and her dwarves, except more than one is grumpy. No one wants to be here but we're stuck with each other and eventually a friendship springs up. It's an unexpected but enduring bond; life lessons are swapped, and a minor off-limits flirtation brews between myself and one of the men. A few years later, I write a book about Heart Attack Club, and then they make a movie out of it: Melissa McCarthy plays me, goofy and rounder than the rest of the women in the movie. The guys are played by the old solids: Kevin Kline, Robert De Niro (he's the grumpiest), Morgan Freeman, George Clooney but with some extra grey, Robert Downey Jr., and Colin Firth. Ryan Reynolds plays the youngest of the club, and the potential love interest.

The movie ends with me and my seven dwarves climbing a mountain, or standing at the edge of the Grand

Canyon, or shoulder-to-shoulder along the railing of a huge ship steaming away from shore. Something that symbolizes that this journey of ours has come to some sort of conclusion. The romance question remains unanswered, because obviously there's a lot of change afoot, but the implication as he looks admiringly at me in the closing scene is clear: anything is possible.

That's how I imagine Heart Attack Club on the way to my first meeting of Heart Attack Club: a band of ragtag oddballs who have faced death, are pissed off and scared, but then discover there's a bigger meaning to it all. There's a plan, shaped by unseen forces. We thought it was the end but in fact it's the beginning. Heart Attack Club will show us our own mortality and also prove *it's all been worth it*.

Heart Attack Club, it turns out, is none of these things.

The chairs are hard and awkward, stackable like the ones in a high school classroom. My rear end starts to feel numb midway through the meeting. The lights are too bright, the air is dry, and we're jammed into a room at the end of a hallway in a local hospital facility. There's coffee but only powdered creamer to go with it, and I drink it just so that I'll have something to do with my hands.

I'm not the youngest, to my surprise. I'm not the only woman. There's a lot more diversity—of gender, age, skin colour, and body type—than I had imagined. The woman across the aisle from me looks like she just came from a competitive tennis match. A teacher from my children's school is here, which explains her sudden absence in recent weeks. There are a lot of South Asian men. There's a guy who can't be a day over twenty-three. He's wearing a Pink Floyd shirt that looks old but is clearly new, probably a buy-one-get-one-free deal on retro T-shirts at Hot Topic. I want to sit next to him and tell him about the time I got too stoned at a Pink Floyd concert the weekend of my high school graduation, passed out in the concession lineup at the intermission, and missed the first twenty minutes of the second half. I bite my tongue. No one wants my stories here.

I was right about one thing regarding Heart Attack Club: there are indeed a lot of grumpy men. The grump level has a direct correlation to the number of grunts they make and eye rolls they offer as we discuss various topics. I sneak peeks at their faces, studying the lines there, the shape of eyebrows and the pressed lips. I wonder what happened to them. Where were they when "it" happened? How many people came to visit them in the hospital? Are they angry? They definitely look angry. Are they actually sad but don't know how to be sad? Are they wondering where the time went and who's the old guy looking back at them when they brush their teeth?

I wonder how many of them have zippered-up chests under their shirts, an ugly line of stitches to close up the necessary incision for open-heart surgery? They have to crack the ribs open to get to the heart. A lot of people don't know that. It's like opening a kitchen cupboard, a hand on adjacent knobs, swinging wide. Then closing the doors again. Then sewing the doors shut, with a warning not to cough hard because cupboard doors can fly open under the right conditions. I remember my father's cupboard-door chest, and know that chances are good that half the men around me have similar.

I wonder, but I don't ask. My usual MO in any new environment—start conversations, find kindred spirits, be grateful for the unexpected twist of fate that has allowed our paths to cross—doesn't work here. No one bonds over surgery war stories. The potential for a minor off-limits flirtation is zero. I can barely get anyone to smile back at me when I say "Good morning" as we arrive and find our seats.

No one even calls it Heart Attack Club, except me, and I don't call it that out loud.

If I'm being precise, I should call it "Heart and Other Associated Maladies and Oddities Club." Take me, for example: I didn't have a heart attack at all, but I'm funnelled into this group because *a cardiac intervention is a cardiac intervention is a cardiac intervention*. I had progressive angina, which doesn't sound very dramatic, but considering I thought I had sore lungs from inhaling too much smoke in the casinos during a trip to Las Vegas, and discovered a month later it was a ninety-nine percent blockage in my left circumflex artery, it's rather overwhelming all the same.

It could have been death: instant, sudden, no-turning-back death, at any moment. It wasn't, but it could have been. In the months after, I obsess about the days leading up to the tipping point: in that last week, when I had to step off the treadmill to let the pain ease and then, like a fool, got right back on, unaware my heart was screaming at me to pay attention. What if the blockage had blown out? What if the remaining one percent of artery space couldn't keep up with the demand? What if I'd had heart tissue death—as anyone with a heart attack will have—that would plague me for the rest of my life?

Or worse, what if I'd had a massive and sudden heart attack while driving my kids to school one day, the car veering off the road, the nose of the car crashing through a fence, the vehicle rolling to a stop as my children wailed, my son climbing over the seat to get my attention, yanking at my sleeve, desperately screaming: "MAMA MAMA MAMA MAMA MAMA."

I can hear him screaming, as though it happened. Sometimes I wake up with a jolt, sweaty and panicked, his *mama mama mama mama* echoing off into fuzzy dreams, the feel of his little hand tugging still at my sleeve. In some other version of our reality, it *has* happened. My cells remember it in some strange multiverse that future physicists will understand only with the help of alien technology. Another good plot for a story, I tell myself, as I push the blankets off my sweaty limbs.

But none of that happened in *this* universe. No ruptured blockage. No careening off the road mid-attack. What happened instead is a litany of good luck, a blessing of careful eyes: A friend watches me struggling at the gym and guilts me into going to the clinic. The doctor asks lots of questions and then guilts me into going to the local ER. (*I don't think it's your heart, but I don't have the machines to say for sure*, he tells me.) The ER finds nothing wrong with me—at first. Three rounds of bloodwork before the problem shows up and then it's like a neon light pointing directly at my heart. *There is no reason for this enzyme to be in your blood unless your heart is in distress*, the ER doctor tells me. Thank goodness they checked it three times, since it was entirely absent in the first two standard rounds of testing.

They transfer me to the regional cardiac care centre. I make jokes with the paramedics, so I know that I'm still *me*: start conversations, find kindred spirits, be grateful for the unexpected twist of fate that has allowed our paths to cross. You know, the usual.

Like most medical things, figuring out the "why" of this blockage is mostly guesswork and statistics. We know that I have a family history of heart disease, we know that my dad died of a sudden heart something-or-other at the age of sixty-seven and my grandfather experienced a stroke at thirty-nine. We know that I smoked for most of my teens and twenties, even again for a few years in my late thirties. My cholesterol is elevated, but barely. In the plus column, all my other numbers are good, reasonable. My resting heart rate is low. My blood pressure is normal. I work out a lot, I routinely hit ten thousand steps a day, I'm strong, and technically I'm young—just a few weeks past the forty mark when this all happens.

And it turns out that the rest of my heart is clear as can be—like a wide-open freeway on a Sunday morning, with nary a car in sight. *The heart of a twenty-year-old,* says the doctor who works the wire through it, pushing dark dye into the veins to explore the offshoots and main highways. I requested the minimum possible amount of sedation during my angiogram so that I could see what was happening and discover what the problem was at the same they did.

There it is, he says, as I hear everyone else in the room inhale. They all spy it at the same time.

When I ask the doctor *Why this one spot?* he shrugs. *There's no way to know, he says. I'd be a very rich man if I could figure that out,* he adds. Could be damage from a virus, years old, way back to when I was a teenager. Could be something that started during pregnancy. Could be a million things. In the simplest terms: something damaged the artery wall and stuff started to stick to the rough spot.

I start to cry, and because I'm lying flat on my back, strapped down tightly with instructions not to move *at all* while this wire runs its way from a puncture hole in my wrist, up my artery, around my shoulder, and into my heart, the tears run silently down the sides of my face, tickling my ears, cooling as they slide down onto my neck. I try not to make any noise. I try not to shiver. I try not to let my inhalations of breath raise and lower my chest at all. I have already caused so many problems, it's important that now, at least, I am a Very Good Patient. It's foolish to make a fuss. This is all my own fault, anyway, isn't it?

They fix my heart in a matter of seconds, and send me home a few days later with a nitro spray, a handful of prescriptions, and instructions to register for my required education and health classes—aka Heart Attack Club—which I do, immediately, like the Very Good Patient that I am.

Heart Attack Club meets two mornings a week to learn important things from nurses and doctors and nutritionists and sports physiologists. We get lessons on common cardiac medications and cholesterol and block-ages and practical stuff about post-heart-attack depression and simple ways to reduce stress and how to stretch out our muscles for working out. Stuff that most of us know already, but we listen anyway, the quiet broken by grumpy grunts and sighing eye rolls. During the sex-after-heart-attack session, I suppress a small giggle—like I'm a kid in health class learning about fallopian tubes and sperm—and the lady next to me looks over, a slight frown on her face. For a split second, a new story emerges: goofy jokester and serious pessimist cross paths at Heart Attack Club and (in between awkward sessions of sex ed for grown-ups and blood pressure checks) somehow become best friends despite their differences. It's *Beaches*, but less beach and more hospital, and each of us will envy the other for the things we find lacking in ourselves. One of us (probably her, because I'm the main character in this story) will end up succumbing to a second round of something vague and not even heart-related, because life is a bitch and you can escape one thing but another thing might yet be lurking, and her death will make me a better person so it's not all in vain. There are laughs, but not too many laughs, and it ends with everyone in the audience crying, heartbroken and ultimately born anew. For a few seconds, my spirits lift.

But my possible new BFF looks away, and even when I try to catch her eye at the end of the session, she steadfastly pretends I don't exist, shuffling out, empty coffee cup left behind on her seat. I pick it up as I pass, and chuck it in the garbage can along with mine, which seems a responsible and Very Good Patient sort of thing to do.

I keep going to Heart Attack Club, getting checkmarks in my attendance book, slotting in the blood pressure checks, the weight checks, the prescription checks. I keep waiting for the unlikely best friend, the crossed path, the kindred spirit. I watch for Morgan Freeman and Kevin Klein.

I want to believe that my heart-attack-that-was-not-a-heart-attack has some meaning, not just an early road sign of my mortality. I want it to be a plot twist, an inciting event, a turn in the story. I want to be able to look backwards from some future point and see that, of course, it had to happen as it did, that life unfolded as it needed to, strange and funny heart included. I want to learn important lessons, evolve, discover that my perspective and priorities have shifted.

But no matter how hard I try, I can't find the narrative that gives it any sense at all. It's a blip, without meaning or shape—and without a reason for it, without a grand purpose, I flounder. I can handle the random event that is not, in fact, random. But a random event with no bigger purpose is evidence of the thing I fear most: that there's no rhyme or reason for anything, that we really are just cosmic dust briefly spending time in a collection of cells that breathe and walk and think, destined inevitably to return to dust.

In the last session of Heart Attack Club, I close my eyes and let the drone of voices melt down into a quiet rumble, like the noise of a river through a forest. I take a deep breath. I start over.

Heart Attack Club is a room full of strangers. Heart Attack Club is messy, grumpy, dull, funny, traumatic, strange, fascinating, unexpected, and the coffee is mostly terrible. It has whatever meaning I give it, whatever lesson I imagine it might. Or none at all. Heart Attack Club, I realize as I walk out the door for the last time, is not an ensemble. It's a solo show. And the grand finale is not at the edge of the Grand Canyon or at the top of a mountain. It's just me, wrestling with myself, finding meaning in the chaos of the everyday when sometimes none will exist at all.

Red Lipstick and
Dresses with Big Skirts

Blue leggings. The revolution began with sapphire blue leggings.

I most likely wouldn't have even bought them, but the store was having a closing-out sale and they'd been marked down several times, clearance on clearance, until the price was only a few dollars. "Why not?" I thought to myself. I could wear them around the house. I added them to the top of a pile of other items I had already settled on.

My wardrobe up to that point included a stable roster of basics. Sweaters with high necks and long sleeves, preferably black. T-shirts with three-quarter sleeves, mostly black but a quiet pastel was okay from time to time. A couple of loose dresses, definitely black, for formal events when absolutely required. Jeans, in dark denim, loose-fitting and high-waisted. Big boxy button-up shirts, mostly black with a few muted plaids for variety.

No shorts. Nothing sleeveless. Zero cleavage. And bright colours? Definitely not.

It wasn't the wardrobe I wanted, but it was the only wardrobe I permitted myself. Black was flattering, which is a kinder way of saying "might make you look thinner," and, as a bonus, was unlikely to draw much attention. The loose jeans and baggy sweaters hid the lumps and bumps—or any shape at all. The combination was very effective for hiding, an invisibility cloak for imperfect bodies. And anyway, I told myself after my kids came along, I was forever getting dirty being down on the floor with them, or splattered by baby food. What was the point of wearing something nice when it would be covered with mushy peas before noon?

But inside, I craved jewel tones, pinstripes, bright florals, and crisp whites. I flipped through high-fashion magazines, in love with the bold jewellery, the dramatic runway shapes, the high-rise heels. I loved tailored men's collared shirts over cropped cigarette pants, cheetah-print miniskirts with pouf-shouldered angora sweaters, and soft chiffon ball gowns. I mooned over vintage party dresses and pin-up-style Mary Jane heels, and I imagined walking along a beach in a flowing caftan over a glamorous plunging bathing suit.

And I promised myself I would indulge. Someday. When my thighs were smaller. When the kids were older. When I had more money, as though buying a red top was somehow more costly than the black one. When I deserved better clothes, I would get them. When I was worth it. Pinky swear.

But my internal dialogue is not entirely to blame. Even if I'd given myself permission for more, it wouldn't have been a simple thing to do. When you're above a size fourteen, it's challenging to fill a closet with anything at all, let alone something beautiful. For most of my teens and twenties, shopping was something I did in two distinct categories: first, with friends in the regular stores in the mall, gushing over the pieces I'd have wanted for myself, living vicariously through their choices; and second, solo at the extremely limited plus-sized retailers that existed at the time.

For years, those plus-sized stores offered dowdy past-your-prime Easter-hued pastels in shapes that were a cross between a shower curtain and a Mongolian yurt, or they were the fashion equivalent of a piercing scream: so loud it couldn't be ignored, even from the other side of a large crowd. These latter options were intended to prove that a lifetime of being fat hadn't squashed one's innate sense of style, confidence, enthusiasm, and excitement. It was all very in-your-face, very "excuse me, of course a size twenty-four can wear a boxy waist-length neon-yellow faux-leather jacket with seventeen decorative zippers and look fabulous" (never minding, meanwhile, that no one at any size looked fabulous in that, ever). Additionally, in a pre-internet world, the options were limited to whatever was close to hand. And what was close to hand was mostly garbage—costly garbage, at that.

But sometime in my midthirties, there was a confluence of factors that altered the clothing landscape for fat women: internet shopping began in earnest, retailers realized there were a host of possibilities between pastel shower curtains and bumblebee jackets, and straight-sized companies discovered they were missing out on a significant demographic and expanded their sizing range.

The lingerie got pretty nice, too. Rather than white, nude, or black, there were bras in every colour, with lace, and bows, and deep front plunges. Silky slips and chemises. Cute nighties that didn't look like something your great-grandmother wore in 1847.

I looked at the new choices with longing. They'd fit, but did I deserve them? Maybe. Maybe if I lost five pounds, or ten. Or fifty. Maybe I'd give myself permission if I managed that.

But then: the blue leggings.

After I got the kids to bed that night, I tried on everything in my big bag of sale finds. Black beach cover-up. Black T-shirt. A new pair of pyjamas, black but dotted with little pink hearts. Big cowl neck sweater. Big turtleneck sweater. Big mock-neck sweater. And, at the bottom of the bag, the half-forgotten electric blue leggings.

I pulled them on with one of the long sweaters, not in an attempt to create an outfit but to see how they fit, envisioning them as an around-the-house thing—something to put on to watch a movie, maybe, or to do one of my yoga videos in my living room. It felt strange. I couldn't remember the last time I'd worn something that hugged my body, something that revealed my shape in any way at all. I moved a little, wiggled, stretched.

"Huh. Comfortable enough," I thought. Hideous to look at, no doubt, but comfortable.

When I turned to see in the mirror, they weren't hideous at all. They looked ... good. In fact, they looked great. They were the brightest of bright blue, a sapphire peacock-feather azure ocean blue that popped against the black of the sweater. I stared at myself in wonder, and then I wore them the very next day. A week later, I had the same pair in both emerald green and fuchsia pink. The revolution had begun.

It might have been better for my budget, and certainly for my minuscule closet space, had the blue leggings never been discovered. Because in the coming years, I didn't just give myself permission to indulge a little bit. Instead, I went on what can only be described as a fashion bender, binge-shopping my way through clothing stores, thrift shops, vintage boutiques, online retailers, and clothing swaps.

All through my early forties, I indulged in almost everything I'd ever admired from afar: a gold sequin wrap dress, a cherry-dotted pin-up skirt with a red crinoline for underneath, dresses with tropical florals, thigh-high striped socks, electric blue high heels. So many bras. And hats. Scarfs. Raspberry tights and Cuban-heeled nude hose with thin black seams up the back. Slips and chemises and garter

belts with stockings built for bigger thighs. Structured jackets and long flowing caftans.

I wore things that were fitted, that didn't hide but accen-
tuated my shape. I bared my cleavage for the first time,
wore push-ups to highlight it. I added chunky necklaces
and long earrings and sparkly purses. After a lifetime of
avoiding dramatic makeup, I fell in love with red lipstick—
and pink, coral, and burgundy, too. I was thrilled when I
had an event to go to, a wedding, a concert, a dinner, a
party, even a professional gathering: they were all oppor-
tunities to ponder what I might wear, which shoes, which
earrings, which outfit to create. I wore dresses for no reason
at all, discovering that they weren't fussy but simple: pop
one over your head and you're ready to go.

Dressing up felt creative, artistic, joyful. It felt like *me* for
the first time. I had gone from hiding quietly in corners to
often being the loudest, brightest thing in the room: a vision
in red lipstick and dresses with big skirts. And I loved it.

It took about a year into the pandemic before I figured
out that my slow-growing malaise was not simply the lack
of social connections, the uncertainty about the future,
the exhaustion of teaching and entertaining children at
home without any normal activities or friends to break
the monotony.

Those things were all hard, of course, and I didn't know
many people who were not experiencing a sort of mental
fatigue over it all.

There was something else going on for me, though, a kind of disconnect between the person I was before and the person I was slowly becoming. I felt blank, flat, colourless. The activities that made me feel like me—attending literary events, going out dancing, hosting big dinners with friends and family—were all impossible. At first, that seemed a sufficient explanation: I missed my old life. But over time I realized I also missed my clothes, desperately, which sounds vain and foolish but true. They had been part of my life in a specific way, a framework through which I had learned to express myself, and, it turned out, to start loving myself.

But now I had defaulted back to wearing the simplest, most shapeless clothing that still remained in my wardrobe. And why not? I had nothing to dress up for, and nowhere to go. Gardening didn't require a sequin dress; playing cribbage with my kids didn't come with a dress code of crinoline and high heels. Why bother fixing my hair, or putting on lipstick? The pretty dresses got pushed further and further back in the closet, while the hoodies and leggings and sneakers came to the front.

It didn't help that my body had changed, too. Thrown overnight out of my usual routines, stuck at home, with my gym closed and activities limited, my body responded to its new conditions quickly. By the end of the first year, most of my clothes didn't fit quite right anymore, or didn't fit at all. I refused to return to the era of punishing myself by suffering through the discomfort of too-small clothes, as some kind of twisted motivation to lose weight, so

I bought a few new things that would fit better. It took me ages to realize that all of the new purchases had one particular feature in common: gone were the florals and stripes and polka dots. Black was back.

That all of this change coincided with entering my late forties, a time when you're already quite likely to experience changes in both your body and your self-perception, certainly did not help. I am not sure there's a good age to weather a pandemic, but I would argue that midlife is not ideal. Time is already a premium at this stage, and the pandemic doubled down on that. Sandwiched between taking care of children and extended family, stuck at home for months on end, attempting to maintain a public career through Zoom events, all while simultaneously trying to keep myself and everyone around me of mostly sound mind and body was … a lot. So much, in fact, that there was no room, or reason, for red lipstick and dresses with big skirts.

But the absence of them was stripping something from my self-identity, the sense of myself as a creature of joy and creativity and light. So I began again with small things: adding a red scarf to go to the grocery store; getting up twenty minutes early to do my hair; putting on bright pink lip gloss even though I'd be wearing a mask over it. Each small addition re-lit another small flame. The fire is not yet as bright as it once was, but it's getting there.

At the time of writing, we've hit the three-year mark, an anniversary that no one wants to celebrate but is hard to ignore. How much the world has changed, and how much we have changed with it. I'm still working to find myself again most days.

But it's happening, by inches. I came home last week with a bright new summer dress. It's yellow and blue and green, covered in 1960s-style mod flowers. It has poufy sleeves and a ruffly hemline, and it's a buttery soft jersey that feels like feathers on my skin. It hasn't been worn anywhere yet—it's still in the brown bag on the floor next to my closet. This dress is the most *me* thing I've purchased in several years, and when I looked at myself in the change room mirror, it was like seeing myself—a new version anyway—for the first time in a very long time.

And those blue leggings? They're still kicking around, and finally living up to the original plan: they are, at long last, something I just wear around the house. They're not fit to wear out in public, and their days are numbered. The fabric is worn thin, the knees bagged out from hundreds of wearings. But I'm not quite ready to give them up yet, not quite ready to say goodbye.

It's not every day that a pair of leggings changes your life.

What Were We Thinking?

Almost everything changes by inches, so slowly that you don't realize it's happening. When children are little, we cannot quite fathom that they won't always be small enough for us to protect. The Earth, too, shifts in slow arcs of evolution, its shape worn down by wind and water, its cycles and seasons unchanged for millennia. We imagine there is always more time to prepare for change and alter course—until suddenly there isn't.

My little brother spots the frog first and calls us over to look, pointing in excitement. A frog? A frog! We all come running. Frogs, we are convinced, would make the best pets—that is, if we can ever catch one. No matter how slow, how careful, how quiet we are, they always manage to hop away, our hands closing on empty air in the spot where they'd just been, grass rustling in their wake.

But this frog is different. He is stuck inside the window well, a semicircle of corrugated tin about half a metre deep, carving out space around the basement window. It's too deep for him to escape on his own. We kneel alongside my brother, the midsummer Ontario sun hot on our little heads. His chubby toddler finger points. "Look," he whispers. "Catch?"

As the oldest kid, this is my job. I reach wide, careful to avoid the tin—the metal gets so hot in the summer sun that it will burn my skin if I brush against it. I close my fingers in slow motion around the frog's body, waiting for him to wriggle and jump.

But he is dry and weightless in my hand, an empty shell, hollow and unmoving. Dead. I drop his little body and it flutters across the rocks like an autumn leaf. I jerk back in surprise; the hot tin of the window well burns the underside of my arm, and I jerk again from the pain, falling backwards onto the grass.

The weather app on my phone tells me it's thirty-nine degrees Celsius, but the large outdoor thermometer hanging in the shade next to my door shows forty-one degrees, and it's not quite eleven in the morning. If I stay out here too long (that is, more than three minutes) I start to feel drunk—dizzy, lightheaded, nauseous. Everything feels bleached-out and paper-thin: the grass under my toes, the leaves on the trees, the dirt in the garden. The heat is oppressive, a physical weight on my body. It is impossible to take a full breath, impossible to move at a normal pace. Every task feels impossible: cooking, chores, sleeping, thinking. I press my hand to my children's foreheads a hundred times a day to make sure they're still hydrated enough to sweat.

This is the tail end of June 2021, and we are midway through a six-day heat wave that is going to get much, much worse before it gets better. It's not really a heat wave at all—which would be uncommon, but not unheard of, here on the west coast of Canada. No, this is a heat dome, a weather term most of us have never heard before this week. Heat builds up under a high-pressure "lid" and can't escape, even at night when temperatures should drop. Each day is disastrously warmer than the last.

Before it eases, more than six hundred people will die throughout the province; most are elderly, living alone and in poverty, without the means to cool off. Ambulance and emergency services will be so overwhelmed that people will wait hours for help after calling 911, adding to the deaths. Crops will shrivel up. A whole town will burn down, dried out like tinder after days on end under some of the hottest temperatures on record in the country.

I try not to think about how bad it is, what it means, as I put the kids to bed with fans running and bottles of water nearby. But after years of canary-in-the-coal-mine warnings on climate change, I know that this is now a legion of canaries: a screeching, terrifying, deadly symphony, and they're all on my doorstep.

...

They say this is a once-in-a-millennium occurrence. But it takes less than half a year for us to be rocked by more extreme weather. That November, we are swamped by torrential rainfall caused by an "atmospheric river"—a weather phenomenon in which a massive corridor of warm moisture-heavy air is carried inland from the Pacific Ocean, leading to flash floods that wipe out bridges, highways, homes, towns. Countless livestock drown on flooded farms. Several people lose their lives, their cars swallowed up in washouts and mudslides.

A month later, we're hit again: a polar vortex brings frigid air from the North Pole, driving overnight temperatures to minus fifteen Celsius near the coast, worse inland, and doubly frigid with the wind chill. I've experienced colder weather in my childhood in Ontario and Alberta, and during winter visits to the Maritimes to see my sister. But this is different. With its typically temperate climate, southern BC's systems aren't designed for this. We have limited city equipment to deal with ice or snow, not enough hydro crews to manage frozen wires. Many people don't even own snow boots, let alone snow tires, and I don't know a single person with a block heater in their car.

Our houses aren't built for these extremes either. Certainly, my eighty-year-old house isn't. In a normal year it's only a problem on a handful of days. But after living through a sixty-degree change in temperature over a span of six months, from forty-plus in summer to minus fifteen in winter, the notion of a "normal year" seems quaint at best, and foolhardy at worst.

During the heat dome, we ran a pair of aging window air conditioners all day and night for weeks (a luxury many people didn't have at all) and the interior of the house still ran into the low thirties. During the vortex, our furnace is hard-pressed to keep up at times, and we pull out rarely used electric blankets. In both instances, we are ready to decamp to the homes of my siblings if necessary, where newer construction and ventilation systems keep things not just tolerable but borderline normal. Most things in life are manageable with the right tools and enough money to purchase them—even, it seems, a climate crisis.

Shortly after the new year, my husband and I start talking about ways we can change the house, within our means, to make it better. Not "granite countertops and fancy appliances" better, but "ready to withstand whatever weather may be coming our way in the future" better. In the middle of a discussion about potential cooling systems, I break down, crying so hard I can barely catch my breath.

"What were we thinking?" I ask between sobs. "What were we thinking?"

My pragmatic partner assumes I am talking about the house, this ancient, imperfect, too-small home that has kept us safely and gratefully housed in a region known for its ongoing housing crisis.

"It's fine. It's great. We can figure this out," he says. "I'm adding a new fan in the attic, okay?"

He knows the fact he can fix and build and wire without help from contractors will ease my stress about what we can or can't afford. But I shake my head, stare at my hands in my lap. It's not the money, or the house, or anything we can repair or renovate.

"I mean the kids. To bring them into … all this. What were we thinking?"

I'm not the first to wonder about the wisdom of having had children in a world that caught fire faster than we expected—or sooner than we wanted to believe, at any rate. I've written about it and lain awake nights pondering it. The question was always pressing and ever-present but still, in most ways, vague: climate change was out there somewhere.

But when I kissed my sleeping children's sweaty foreheads in the middle of the heat dome, the question was on my lips. And when I broke down over a conversation about cooling pumps, about the privilege to even have such a conversation, it was impossible to ignore. It's a question without an answer, really. I simply have to wrestle with the grief that I am in part responsible for a world that is no longer stable enough for them to inherit in safety. We all are.

There's a series of trails through a ravine near my house, which permits me the illusion of being in some far-flung forest, miles from the city. Midwinter, during a walk on a misty-grey day, I hear the distinctive croak of a frog. It takes me by surprise and I pause, standing still to listen for it again. It's somewhere to my left, in a jumble of fallen logs, decomposed leaves, and pockets of rainwater.

He croaks again, and then again. Is this the right time of year for a frog to be awake? Isn't it too early, not warm enough? I have a sudden urge to find him, catch him up in my hands and carry him home. Frogs would make the very best pets, after all—if you could catch one. I am hit with the visceral ghost-memory of a dried-out husk of a frog in my hand.

How he must have suffered, trapped there for days without water in the hot summer sun. If only we'd found him sooner, I think, an echo of childish grief. Surely we'd have saved him, if we'd known what was coming, rescued him if we'd realized in time. Maybe. I hope so. But it seems it is easy to believe there's still time to play, even when it is clear: there is no more time at all.

My Brief but Fruitful Career as a Smut Peddler

For several years, while my kids were at school all day learning how to read and running around the playground at recess, I was at home doing dishes, folding laundry, and writing filthy erotic short stories under several pen names for seventy-five dollars a pop. When I told someone I was busy working on a freelance job, it was equally likely that I meant I was writing a profile for a local business magazine or crafting an X-rated fiction about naked people doing fun and terrible things to each other.

I was a peddler of smut, a purveyor of sex, a teller of tawdry tales. And I was damn good at it. I've never added this to my LinkedIn profile, which is a shame, but it's tough to find the right words to describe this role, wedging it somewhere in between "staff reporter" and "school volunteer." Also, most people don't think too highly of erotica. But I was proud of the work I did, and I still am today.

What I heard from my editor and subsequently from the readers was always the same: This feels real. This feels like something that could happen to a normal person on any random day of the week. This feels like something that could happen to *me*—and it's very, very hot.

My stories were full of regular people: quirky characters with back stories (sometimes only hinted at, but there all the same) who felt uncertainty, shyness, desire, excitement. I wrote about imperfect bodies living in average homes doing normal jobs. I wrote about long-time couples and new friends and sometimes strangers, about threesomes and foursomes and more-somes, and light kink and serious kink and no kink at all. I wrote about gentle sex and rough sex and long sessions that included hours of foreplay and quickies in the laundry room. My stories had skilled lovers and inexperienced ones, and people who fumbled with their clothes and dropped vibrating toys on wood floors. There was laughter and shy smiles and sweaty bodies and groaning and spanking and ratty old pyjamas and beautiful lacy garments.

Whatever else these vignettes included, I stayed in my lane: they were always told from a cisgendered heterosexual woman's perspective. But from that starting point they filled the full spectrum of possibility.

And I always, always, always wrote about consent: a brief pause for a conversation, a verbal confirmation, an agreement, sometimes even a formal contract that ultimately asked, Do we both (or all) want this? The answer was always an enthusiastic yes—*hell, yes*—we really really do. These passages, whether explicit or implied, were the real reason people liked my stories, I think. They were a glimpse of something that many women rarely, if ever, have: a sense that their needs are of equal importance and that they can be both sexual and safe at the same time.

Because you can buy all the lingerie in the world, stock up on handcuffs, learn how to striptease, but enthusiastic consent? Turns out, that's one of the most erotic things of all.

The question everyone is most curious about, when they first hear about this foray into erotica, is how much of the content from those stories was drawn from experience and how much from imagination. I've rarely written in my real-world essays, under my real-world name, about my own real-world love life (save for a few pieces here and there about first heartbreaks and old romances) and I don't intend to start now. It is one of the few parts of my life that I haven't mined deeply, the way I have with my body or motherhood or any of the other themes on which I so frequently find myself preoccupied. Perhaps one day, when I am so close to the end of things that it no longer matters what I reveal about my own secrets (and other people's secrets, by extension), I'll write some steamy tell-all memoir, but until then, that part of my private life shall remain, mostly, private.

I will say that I've probably had a more exciting sex life than anyone looking at me in the grocery store lineup—with my hair in a bun, a hole in the knee of my leggings, oversized tote dangling off my shoulder—might guess at first glance. More exciting than even my friends would guess.

But I've come to discover that's often the case: the most boring people you know—the ones that you'll never see on the cover of a magazine, the ones with nerdy hobbies and weird hair, the fat ones, the lady who volunteers at the animal shelter—are probably having a lot of fun in their private time. (Seriously, if you're looking for enthusiastic, friendly, kinky people? Try the comic shop or a *Star Trek* convention or the adults hanging out at the Lego store on new release day, before you hit up the club or a dating app.)

I was also a slow bloomer, in deed if not in thought, and a private one at that. I was nearly out of high school before I dated at all, and through my twenties I had a few torrid but hidden affairs. If I knew you at university or in the years thereafter and I told you I couldn't hang out on the weekend because I was going to study or do laundry? Sorry. I probably lied to you.

Why? Who knows. There was no reason to be secretive; there was nothing illicit or illegal going on. But I never talked about these relationships, or even acknowledged they existed. They were all mine, something for me alone, and I hoarded the secret of them like a dragon on a gold pile. I became an expert at playing innocent when friends described certain horizontal activities. "What, people do that?" I'd ask, all aflutter, tittering as though I'd never heard the like, while knowing all along that I'd done exactly that thing myself.

In retrospect, it's clear to me that my secrecy was wound up in body shame and sexual guilt and kink and identity, along with a sense that my job was to help other people with *their* relationship woes, not talk about mine. But at the time I told myself it was my own beeswax and no one else's, and that was that.

Around the same time that I was writing erotica in my suburban basement, I spent a year or two selling sex toys. This was one of those home-party companies, except instead of selling food storage or makeup, I was offering vibrators and dildos. I'd show up to a house full of women, a suitcase of sex toys in hand, and then I'd deliver a fantastic spiel, pointing out the unique features of each item one by one. The gist of the speech, if you condensed it down, was: Listen, ladies, sex is good and healthy and important, whether it's by yourself or with other people, and life is too short to feel weird about your desires and your fantasies. Now check out the ten modes of vibration on this rabbit. Also, did you know that you can use an open-ended cock sleeve to make blow jobs easier if you're prone to gagging? And don't mix silicone lube with silicone toys; water-based only, unless it's glass.

I said things to strangers at those parties that I couldn't have said in front of most people in any other environment.

I became the boldest, most comfortable, most kinky version of myself. And the parties were a hoot. People got loud, the jokes got dirty, and everyone had fun.

But the best part for me was the one-on-one chats that happened after the big show, where I'd take the orders from the women privately, in a separate room down the hall, behind a closed door.

There were always a few who were happy to share with the whole group what they planned to buy and didn't mind regaling a crowd of friends (and sometimes strangers) with their sex-toy stories, but most preferred privacy to make their orders. And to ask questions.

And oh, they had questions. About the toys, of course, but about so much more. About their own bodies, about their partners' bodies. About their experiences and identities and insecurities and hang-ups. About whether or not they were normal. I had women of every age, every size, every sexual orientation, every skin colour ask: Is that okay? Is that weird? Am I allowed to like that, do that, want that?

And what one person deemed vanilla another might see as kinky—particular positions, even, had been imbued with meaning, from loving to degrading, though the conclusion of which was which, and why, varied from one person to another. And most people weren't even sure why they felt the way they did.

I discovered that almost all of us have shame about sex that is so deeply rooted in our psyches we no longer know where it came from. Sometimes from parents or religion. Sometimes from early experiences. Sometimes from television or books or movies. Often, it seems as though it emerges from nowhere at all.

I discovered that the moment you eased someone's shame, even a tiny bit, in its place grew joy. And giving someone joy gave me joy, and lessened my own shame, too. Those private conversations were full of learning, and unlearning, for the customer and for myself.

Who knew that selling sex toys would lead to epiphanies?

It's a different world now than it was when I was growing up. Finding sex-positive resources is only a few clicks away. Though the internet brings its own problems, and plenty of them, I confess I rather envy teenagers and young adults this magical portal that helps them find themselves, and like-minded community—a clearing house of resources that we so totally lacked. It's hard not to wonder how much earlier I might have shed my own kink shame, if I'd had access to Tumblr in my twenties rather than my forties, even though I began with a positive foundation when it came to sex.

My first significant exposure to human sexuality was a copy of *The Joy of Sex* on my godparents' bookshelf when I was about ten. They had a small guest room whose walls were covered with bookshelves. One night, as my godmother was helping me settle in, the word *sex* jumped out at me from the spine of one of the books. It was like one of those neon lights with a big arrow pointing to it and bulbs flashing on and off around it. Impossible to ignore.

I waited till everyone was asleep, turned on the lamp, and plucked the book from the shelf, memorizing exactly where it had been and how far it was pulled out before I touched it. I knew I would have to return it to its exact position so my exploration would go unnoticed.

I flipped the pages, mesmerized. This was the original *Joy of Sex*, also known as "the one with the hairy hippies." The simple illustrations were happy, sensual, carefree, and erotic, somehow all at once. It was a total revelation. I wasn't old enough to be aroused but I was something: curious, titillated, totally fascinated. I am not the only person of my generation to have had this experience; I've heard others talk about finding a copy of this book while babysitting or tucked into a parent's bedside table. I am convinced it had a special magic that, once encountered, lingered in the psyche. It embedded in me a deep sense that sex was supposed to be fun, that it was natural, and normal, and bodies were meant to be celebrated. Though the ensuing years would warp that memory with all sorts of limits and rules, uncertainty and myths, the core of it must have persisted in some small way.

Why else would I have been willing to go into people's houses with a cache of dildos and stand in front of them talking about the best ways to clean your sex toys? Somewhere deep down, I always knew that sex was meant to be, as the title of that book had long ago suggested, joyful.

But it wasn't until those long, question-filled conversations I had with customers that I really began to shed my own useless layers of shame and guilt. When someone asked me if they were weird, it turns out I wasn't just answering them—I was also speaking to some younger version of myself who had wondered, so many times, if I was weird, and if I was allowed to do that, like that, want that?

Like most things in life, this process is a work in progress. But it's one that might never have begun at all, if it weren't for my brief but fruitful career as a peddler of smut. Maybe one of these days I'll write a whole book of erotica—under my very own name.

Crop Circles

I grip the handles of the chair while the doctor stands over me, pressing the tip of the needle into my scalp, lightning-fast like the needle on a sewing machine. Prick, prick, prick, prick, prick. Pause. Prick, prick, prick, prick. Pause.

I try to control myself but can't, cursing under my breath the entire time.

"Fuck. Fuck. Jesus. Fuck. FUCK." My eyes are squeezed shut and my cheeks are wet with tears. "Don't move," I think to myself, stay still and don't move. And then I think, as I always do: "I'm never doing this again. I'm never doing this again. I am never, ever, ever, doing this again."

It's not worth it. This is the most painful thing I've ever felt. More painful than the needles that were pushed into the base of my spine for my epidurals so I could be cut open to deliver my babies, more painful than the metal staples that pulled too tight on my C-section incision, more painful than the back injury from a car accident, more than broken toes, than the fall I took on icy bricks that left me black and blue for a month. I've experienced plenty of pain in my life, but this process—steroid injections into patches of bare skin on my scalp—is by far the worst.

"Almost there," the doctor says several times, dragging out the "ah" at the start of *almost* so each word is extra long. "Ahhhhlmost there." Prick, prick, prick, prick, prick.

"And there we go. Done." He swipes some gauze across the last injection site; I catch the flash of red blood on the white cotton as he turns to dispose of it.

When I let go of the armrests, my fingers are numb from the intensity of my grip. I'm embarrassed and sheepish now. "Sorry for the f-word. Again."

He smiles. "We'll see you in September for the next round, okay?"

I've already forgotten that I promised myself just thirty seconds ago that I would not, in fact *could not*, do this ever again. The pain has receded now, leaving in its wake an uncomfortable heat in my scalp, a flush of adrenalin in my tingling limbs, and a slow-blooming headache that will last for the rest of the day. I can manage it. I can do this one more time.

"For sure," I say. "See you then."

It's worth it. Anything is worth it, to get back my hair. My beautiful hair.

...

I hate my hair. I'm fifteen and everything on my body feels awkward and my hair is no exception: It's frizzy and enormous and unmanageable and ugly. It's not straight, unless I straighten it, and not curly, unless I curl it—and I can't do either of these things because there's just too much hair altogether and either task will take more than an hour, never mind that managing the back without help is a fool's errand. Blow-drying requires Herculean upper-arm strength, but if left to air-dry it will still be damp in the afternoon. There is no style or length that works for me: If I let it grow long, I look like a sister wife. Shoulder-length becomes a Cleopatra wedge, a fluffy pyramid that sits on my head like a hat. Short? Who knows. I don't dare risk it, but I'm pretty sure it would come out like a dandelion gone to seed: a fluffy round circle prone to destruction in the breeze. It will be another twenty-five years before YouTube hairdo tutorials exist. For now, it's just me, a brush, a mirror, and a lot of tears.

When I was little, my hair garnered lots of compliments. I had a shiny bob, like a miniature Dorothy Hamill but sandy blond, with bangs so thick they barely moved. But somewhere between preschool and high school, my hair changed, slowly growing in frizzy rather than shiny, darkening in spots, lightening in others, developing random cowlicks that pushed sections up into weird little twists, bangs fluffing up every which way.

I do my best to keep it tidy, controlled, and presentable for school. Most days this means braids or a ponytail or brushing the top half as tight and smooth as can be and clipping it back in a barrette. This latter option pulls at my temples and gives me a headache, but it's necessary. I don't want to look unkempt or lazy. I'm already the chubbiest girl in my high school, so my hair is just one more way my body doesn't meet expectations. Being *tidy and controlled and presentable* is a survival skill.

For my high school graduation photos, I am determined to have decent hair. I spend three hours slowly brushing the wet strands until it dries, smooth and flat. By some miracle, it is perfect. Shiny and straight as a pin. It's one of the only photos from high school that I don't immediately destroy or hide in the bottom of a shoebox in the back of a closet.

A few years later, in my early twenties, I dye it all dark. I am shooting for a glossy mahogany, envisioning a sleek, bouncy wave and a cute rolled fringe, a secret homage to Bettie Page, whose risqué pin-ups in bullet bras and a perfect hairdo somehow manage to exude sex and glamour and joy all at once. Instead, it comes out a flat brown-black, dull and fuzzy. I continue with the ponytails and braids. It's fine, though; it was silly to think I could copy something *sexy and glamorous and joyful*. I don't try to dye it back to blond, and the brunette, as awful as it is on me, sticks around for nearly a decade. All the better to stay hidden, to be unobtrusive, to not draw attention to myself.

It's my hairdresser who finds the bald spots.

"Okay, honey, I don't want to freak you out, but …" She trails off, hands slowing.

Sometime in my thirties I went back to blond and figured out how to do something with my hair. YouTube had arrived, along with curlers and straighteners and blow-dryers that were easier to use and didn't burn my hair into frizz. It took time to learn, but it worked: my hair looked good. Some days, it looked great, actually. For the first time since early childhood, people exclaimed over my hair: *It's so thick, it's so pretty, I love it, I wish I had your hair, I'm jealous.* Strangers in the grocery store line commented on it. For once, I was good enough at something that other people—other women in particular—might envy me. Me! It was a heady novelty. I hadn't had the body or the wardrobe or the makeup skills or the career, but now I did have something: I had *good hair.*

I don't want to be vain, but it turns out that in this regard, I am very vain indeed. Maybe that's why it happened. Maybe it was a punishment for enjoying the attention, for permitting myself this one vanity.

"I don't want to freak you out," my hairdresser continues. "But ... did you know you have some spots back here with no hair?"

No. No, I did not know. I reach up and back with both hands, running my fingers through my hair to find whatever it is she has spied. My fingertips slide over a bare spot, and then another, and another.

"Oh my god," I say. "Oh my god."

She uses my phone to take a few photos and I am totally unprepared for what they reveal: three large spots, completely bald. Not thinning, not patchy. Bald. One has a mottled pinkish appearance, but they are all smooth, not even baby fuzz, and almost completely symmetrical and round. Later, I will describe them by their size: there's the one that is a little bigger than a toonie, the one that's like an Oreo, and the one that's the bottom of a muffin. I don't know why these three things come to mind—coin, cookie, muffin—but I reference them in that way for the next several years. None of them are enormous, but in that moment they seem huge; they look to me as big as saucers, the size of dinner plates, so big they might take over my whole head.

I start to cry.

"Okay, I see this a lot, it's not uncommon," my hairdresser says, reassuring me. "There could be a lot of reasons for it." She tells me I'm lucky because I've got so much hair, and the spots are mostly hidden by the way the rest of it falls over the bare patches. I hadn't even noticed it was missing, she points out. Which is true, but also strange. How did so much hair disappear without any evidence? Without clumps of it in my brush, or in the shower, or on my pillow in the morning?

We decide not to do anything that day after all—no treatments, no cuts, no brushing. I'm terrified to even touch it, afraid I'll make it worse.

But as I drive myself home, I'm more terrified by the fact that I don't know what has caused it. I've lost hair before: during pregnancy, my hormones led to some random and excessive shedding, an all-over thinning. A few years later, undiagnosed severe anemia did the same.

I wasn't bothered, though; if anything, it made my hair more manageable to have slightly less of it.

But this is something different. This is not thinning, or breakage, or damage. This hair is gone, leaving blank spots on my head like the flattened crop circles that appear overnight in a farmer's field. Who knows how or why or, worst of all, if it will happen again.

My doctor says it looks like alopecia, an autoimmune condition that causes hair loss, and she sends me to a dermatologist, who confirms at a glance: yes, definitely alopecia. I already know what this means, because a friend of mine has had it since our teen years, juggling periods when the condition was dormant and periods of near-total hair loss, including eyelashes and eyebrows.

By the time I'm at the dermatologist's office, I've managed to rally myself into comedy and courage. I've stopped asking my sister and my best friend to take magnified photos of the bald spots in the sunshine, then zooming in on the images, looking for evidence of fine baby hairs that might indicate regrowth. I've made an informative, revealing post on Facebook in which, as always, I make myself the butt of the joke: I tell the story of their discovery like it's a stand-up comedy bit. No one knows I cried so hard that first day that I broke blood vessels in my face, a fine wash of pink freckles across my cheeks for days after. I call the bald spots my crop circles, to make other people feel more comfortable, to suggest that it's no big deal. It is important to be brave, especially about something that is not really important in the grand scheme of things. It's just hair after all, and I will be fine. Right?

The dermatologist tells me he'd like to start with some injections and add a daily topical prescription cream. "Sure," I say, nonchalant, as though I'll go along with this plan but am not invested in the outcome.

But I am, of course, deeply invested in the outcome. He could have told he'd have to perform surgery, draw blood, maybe take my pinky finger in sacrifice, and I'd have said "Sure." Whatever it takes. Anything.

A few moments later, I am gripping the armrests for the first time, eyes shut tight, tears pouring down my face. Prick, prick, prick, prick, pause.

That initial round, I let only a single f-bomb escape, biting my lips through the rest of the process. I am steely and determined. I can do this. I can definitely do this. It's worth it.

"Okay, so the cream every day," he says, handing me a slip of paper with the prescription on it. "And let's do the next injections in eight weeks."

"Oh! We do this again? The shots?" It hadn't occurred to me this was a multi-step process, having interpreted the treatment as a one-and-done cure.

"Oh yeah, we'll do it a few times likely. Depends on how you respond, what kind of growth we see. Everyone is different."

I pray that there will be so much new hair by the next visit, that maybe he'll tell me I'm cured, forever, the first person in the universe to reverse alopecia.

But when I come back in eight weeks, there's nothing, not even a fuzz to suggest the injections occurred at all.

I am forever preaching to others about self-love. No one cares about your stretch marks, go swimming. Don't save your favourite jewellery for a special occasion, wear it today. Stop buying black clothes and put on a red dress, or blue high heels, or rainbow leggings. Just be you!

But here I am, hiding out, tearful, anxious about a trio of bald spots on my head. I had convinced myself that I had embraced the real me these last few years, that I had learned to love myself, but the truth is that I had learned to love what I learned to do with myself. I hadn't stopped trying to fix my hair, I had learned how to manage it. I didn't love my imperfect self; I had only learned to like the ways I could hide that imperfect self with some curling rods and hairspray.

So much for self-actualization and shedding unrealistic expectations. I've been revealed as the scam artist that I am, shouting from my pulpit about body image and the beauty myth while still buying into all of it.

I feel both overwhelming relief and a strange shame when my hair finally begins to grow again, coming in darker and curlier than the surrounding hair. I am so grateful it has returned, but simultaneously embarrassed at the discovery of how much it meant to me to lose it.

Alopecia is, for most, a recurrent condition: it will likely reappear at random intervals for the rest of my life. I wish I could say that I'll be unphased by how it *looks*, or if other people notice, and I'll shrug it off, no big deal. This seems admirable, but unlikely.

We grow up being told directly and indirectly, in a million small ways, that hair is a very big deal, but also not to admit to it. It's a sign of femininity, or of youth, or the lack thereof, and we know that our beauty and attractiveness and certainly our worth will be judged by this crowning feature. But when we get upset with a bad haircut, or stress about the grey coming in, or panic over thinning hair, we're told we're being foolish: goodness, it's just hair, after all.

It is just hair, this is true. But it is also, clearly, so much more.

part 3

The Uncertain Path Ahead

Finding My Way Home

The large brown envelope followed me from place to place, home to home, for more than twenty years. In university, it sat tucked into a bookshelf in my miniature dorm room, wedged between a course catalogue and student loan documents. For a while, it lived in a filing box where I saved the most important stories I had worked on during my years as a journalist, a random interloper in a stack of newspaper clippings. At some point after my youngest child was born, the envelope made its way to the kitchen, where it lived at the bottom of a stack of rotating household bills for more than ten years.

Inside was my father's most important wish, the topic of the last conversation I recall having with him before he died. A stack of partially completed paperwork that described who I am, and where I come from. Paperwork that asked: *Who are your people?*

This is how you locate yourself as an Indigenous person in Canada. Who are your people? Where are you from? Who are your kin? It's how individuals and communities understand their connectedness and relationships.

It's also the question that, when explored deeply enough, helps catch out the fakers and frauds—"pretendians"—who claim a particular heritage for all manner of reasons, most often for some benefit in their careers. But for people who have lost their connections or their link to community, it can be a question of uncertainty, even anxiety: Who am I really? Who claims me? Where do I belong, and do I deserve to belong at all?

If you ask me who my people are, my gut answer is: my siblings. There are four of us, our lives closely interwoven. I cannot fathom a world without them, though I know that one of us will go first, someday, and one of us will be the last remaining. Even writing these words makes my throat close, my eyes blur with tears. How could the universe continue to exist, absent one of us?

We were our own small island nation in a childhood that saw us transplanted like nomads from one side of the country to the other, more than once. I attended six schools—or was it seven?—between kindergarten and high school graduation, in three different provinces. My dad's family was on the West Coast, and my mother's in rural Quebec. I knew that our extended clans on both sides cared about me, and that I had aunts and uncles and cousins and second cousins twice removed sprinkled all over the place who wished to know me, but our paths crossed infrequently at best.

The only constant was my immediate family, my sister and my brothers. They were my people. They still are today.

Unlike many people disconnected from their Indigenous communities, I knew exactly who I was growing up, even though I was far away. How could you not in my house, filled as it was with art and family heirlooms: carvings, paintings, jewellery. There's a photo of my mother nursing me with my father's button blanket on display on the wall behind her, its rows of white buttons on a navy and red background a stark contrast to the 1970s apartment. The woven basket in which I was carried home from the hospital sat on a shelf alongside other baskets, hooked rugs, and abalone shells in every house we lived in.

But this was my connection to community: images and objects framed and hanging on the walls, a culture and people that existed sometime else and somewhere else. It was static, something I observed from the outside.

From time to time, particularly during my early twenties, I'd attend events with my father, escorting him to birthdays and funerals. I'd sit, counting the minutes till we could leave, feeling out of place and lonely, while my dad chatted up cousins or an old friend of his parents or someone with whom he'd once fished a season on a commercial boat. I had learned growing up to measure by degrees of relatedness: first cousin, second cousin. If I used the term *aunt*, it meant my mother's sisters and only my mother's sisters. But here, these terms meant something else, and I struggled to remember who was who or how we were linked. My dad would disappear into the crowd, asking elders about old family stories, collecting information for an expansive family tree he was obsessed with. I'd do my best to hide, though I watched with envy as others in the room laughed, danced, drummed. If someone smudged, I stayed well back, not allowing myself to wash in the smoke. My feet would tap under my chair, and my nose would lift to the scent, but I stayed where I was at the edges, filled with an ache that was both foreign and familiar at the same time, a deep loneliness that had no name.

As children, my sister and I made up long, complicated stories while playing with dolls, pretending we were refugees coming to North America: the closet became the hold of a large ship, the swing set became a train. We were always escaping, seeking a new life. Most often, I imagined we were Jewish. Later, I went through a phase of devouring chapter books about Mennonite girls. I had a friend on my street whose family was Greek Orthodox and I loved sitting in their kitchen, listening to her grandmother speak a jumble of English and words I didn't understand while she cooked food I didn't recognize, images of saints looking down on us. I spent hours reading old *National Geographic* magazines, swept away by the stories and photos of small groups living in relative isolation in the Himalayan mountains or an Amazon river basin, their traditions and clothing and jewellery as strange to me as if they had come from another planet. For years I wished that, at a minimum, I might become Catholic so that I could go to a school with the word *heart* in the name and wear the same outfit as everyone else and attend church at night with hundreds of candles.

I was in my late thirties before I realized that all these obsessions and imaginary games and daydreams were connected. They were all ways of *belonging*, simply by birth. What would that be like? To have to do nothing at all, other than be born, to be part of a group? To a child who grew up all over, whose people were her nuclear family, where traditions lived mostly as art on the walls and as secular versions of Christian holidays, it had obviously become a central question, a fantasyland to dream about.

I still cannot quite imagine this kind of belonging—automatic, by birthright—though it seems I crave it as much as I ever did.

I laughed out loud the first time I saw the title of Indigenous author and playwright Drew Hayden Taylor's book *Funny, You Don't Look Like One*. Blond and fair-skinned, Taylor does not "look like one." In his book, he talks about being invited to speak at various events and showing up to baffled organizers who thought that they had booked someone who would look, well, a little more *Native*.

I don't look like one either. No surprise, considering the mix: I'm Irish, a titch Hawaiian (my great-great-great grandfather), Norwegian, English, and, to people's endless surprise, Indigenous. More specifically, we are Kwakwaka'wakw (Kwak'wala-speaking people), one nation of which today is Da'naxda'xw First Nation, my father's band. I have never lived there, but my father's ashes were scattered in the inlet, a request he made before his death.

Taylor grew up with his people. I grew up with an *idea* of people. I can tell you the name of our nation, but my pronunciation will always be a little bit wrong and my voice goes up at the end, like a question mark, as though I am already second-guessing myself before the words are out of my mouth.

There's something about finding yourself past the halfway mark on your own expiry date that forces you to reconsider who you are and where you're going. Sometime in the first summer of the pandemic, eight years after my father's death, and four years after a close brush with my own mortality, I pulled out the big brown envelope and started my reconsidering.

The paperwork inside was so old that the forms were long outdated, and had been filled in by hand; I recognized my father's handwriting, a scratchy sharp cursive. I went online and found the newest versions of the same document, in downloadable and edit-ready PDFS: the

Application for Registration on the Indian Register and for the Secure Certificate of Indian Status.

Most people are registered for status at birth if their parents are registered. But there are also people who were never registered due to laws that precluded them from status, or when status laws were applied in inequitable ways. Women who married white men, for example, were stripped of their status, while Indigenous men who married white women would confer status onto their spouses. In a single family, you could have a sister without status and a brother with it, their children and grandchildren then continuing to either have or not have status, depending on which sibling they descended from. Same-generation cousins might find that some of them had status and could be members of their home band, while others did not have status. Others lost their status and gained "full citizenship" after earning a university degree or serving in the armed forces or various other enfranchising activities. (The concept of "status" is further complicated by the fact that it is itself an imposed colonial concept: a government body still decides who is and is not status based on laws created in Ottawa, but this is a topic that could fill an entire book.)

It's taken a long time to rectify the equity issues enshrined in earlier versions of the Indian Act, a multi-step process that saw changes one by one over several decades. My father applied for his status in the 1990s. It was a complicated and paper-heavy process in a pre-internet era, evidenced by the folder of documentation I inherited—letters from his band, birth certificates, back-and-forth correspondence from what was then known as Indian Affairs. I am sure the red tape must have slowed down a great many people, but my father was persistent.

Once his was complete, and his status card was proudly tucked into his wallet on top of his driver's licence in a place of priority, the next step was to register each of his four children, who were, by then, teenagers.

As the oldest, I was first. It was a process I resisted from the start.

My father and I had a challenging relationship, one that I will be sorting out for the rest of my life. I am not interested in exploring the nooks and crannies of that on the public page to the degree I have explored it in my own heart. It's enough to say that he struggled to be a parent because he was missing the tools needed to do the job, though it has taken me a long time to come to that understanding. There's a reason it's called intergenerational trauma.

I wasn't home much in my last years of high school and I moved out at eighteen, eager to be independent. So when the topic of applying for my status came up, I would nod and smile, avoid and ignore. It was relatively easy to dodge, despite his authoritarian approach to fatherhood, with vague promises and changing the topic, especially as I got older and my time at home increasingly infrequent.

My refusal to do the paperwork was, I realize now, a way to exert some control and autonomy, something I had grown up with so little of. I had never been good enough, smart enough, pretty enough. Now I would not be Indian enough either. I didn't do it because it was important to him.

That I carted the envelope through more than a dozen moves over the coming twenty years suggests that it was, just maybe, important to me, too.

I was never ashamed of who I was, though I knew I was supposed to be. Even the littlest children on a playground know it is better to be the cowboy than the Indian.

In high school, a kid who lived up the street from me paused near my locker, and warned me that there had been a drunk guy in my driveway when he'd walked past that morning. A drunk Indian, to be precise, emphasis on the word *Indian*, who had been sniffing around the cars.

The "drunk Indian" was my grandfather, who had come to live with us a few years prior, and whose stumbling gait was the result of a massive stroke he'd suffered in his late thirties, which left him with slightly lopsided movements for the rest of his life.

In a social studies class, during a study on "ancient" Indigenous cultures, a fellow student made a comment about lazy Indians. A hot-cold flush went over my body, and I started to argue with them, debating the point as though it were an academic exercise. When the bell rang, I left the class in a rage.

During a Christmas dinner with a boyfriend's extended family, someone made a joke about building a liquor store outside the entrance to a reservation, a guaranteed model for business success. My boyfriend let them chatter, then when they had sufficiently outed themselves, he filled them in on my family history. The room went silent, until someone finally announced with great cheerfulness that they had known a "Native guy" once, and gosh, he was really great—one of the good ones, you know.

These kinds of conversations have happened countless times because I am invisible. My blond hair and fair skin make me "safe," a person that others assume will most certainly have the same perspective as they do, a person who might be worried about a drunk man in my driveway or laugh about the prospect of opening a liquor store outside a reservation.

As uncomfortable as that is, it's nothing compared to what most Indigenous people—the ones who "look like one"—experience daily in schools, stores, hospitals, on the street, at the bank, everywhere.

I have been exposed to the discrimination against Indigenous people in this country, but like the art hanging on the walls of my childhood home, it is something observed, and rarely lived.

My author bio has never included this information. I seldom mention it, even when asked. The publishing world has only recently begun to make room—a very small amount of room—at the edge of the stage for Indigenous writers. My fear of taking up space that doesn't belong to me, that someone else might need more, is deeply rooted; I am terrified that someone might accuse me of being yet another pretendian, of race-shifting, of accessing resources that I don't deserve. Once, at a reading, a cousin of my father's asked me if I might someday write about "your Native history," and the adrenalin that spiked through my body was like a bolt of lightning. What if someone in the audience thought I was yet another blond lady claiming a great-great-great-great-great-great-grandmother who was a Cherokee princess? I answered by saying that probably someone else was better placed for that than I was, and moved on to another topic.

Somewhere along the way I convinced myself that my individual experience was not an "Indigenous experience" and that my visible privilege, my European ancestry, and my lack of lived community, overrode any right to the other parts of my heritage. It has taken me nearly fifty years to realize that I have swallowed whole the same myth that most in Canada have: that Indigenous people in this country are a monolith, alike in all ways. If my experience didn't look a certain way, if my people wouldn't know me if they saw me, I didn't count.

I understand now that if I am disconnected from this part of my family, it is by design. Disconnection was the goal all along. Residential schools, the Sixties Scoop. Outlawing potlatch and powwow and language and ceremony. Indian agents and the Indian roll, status and loss of status. It all had the same intent: to break apart community, to remove people from each other.

On a cultural level, I could see this as the tragedy it is, and believed that people should reconnect, find family, learn their histories. But on a personal level, I used my disconnection as overwhelming evidence that I personally did not belong, and I should not try to. It was all right for others to yearn for and seek community, but not me.

My siblings have much less conflict about their identity. Although it's complicated for them, too, who they are and what they do don't often overlap the way they do for me in the literary world.

I envy them that space to just be. Two of them have been taking Kwak'wala language classes with elders, learning words that I'm quite sure my father didn't know—but also hearing stories, listening to elders, and even accidentally encountering long-distant relations. My sister did not grow up smudging but taught herself how—good medicine for spirit, mind, and body. One of them has helped to craft policy in their workplace around issues of reconciliation. Our children take part in programs at their schools organized by the Aboriginal resource programs; one of the most important people in my son's elementary education was his resource worker, a generous Saulteaux woman from Saskatchewan with whom he ate most of his lunches for several years. This thread of our family history is wound through the varied and complicated braid that is our lives in countless ways.

Yet, when asked by a magazine if there were any Indigenous writers in an anthology I edited, for a review they were interested in doing, I hesitated—and then identified the contributors in the book, but not myself. When I set up my profile for the national arts grants funding program, I clicked "no" under the self-identification category. On Twitter, I was taken to task for using the term *intergenerational trauma* in a particular context; rather than dive into an explanation about my history, I simply bowed out of the conversation and deleted my tweet.

And when I knew I could access a COVID-19 vaccine at an early clinic specifically for Métis, Inuit, and status and non-status First Nations individuals, I spent weeks agonizing over whether or not it was right and ethical to do so, despite the fact that some of the known health complications that impact Indigenous people at higher rates had already come home to roost in my body. My risk was higher, by genetic heritage, no matter where I grew up or the colour of my hair, but I hesitated to give myself permission.

I dared not take up any room, anywhere. Who was I to ask for such a thing? Who was I to ask to belong in these ways, in any way at all?

In the years after my father passed away, the big brown envelope slowly made its way closer and closer to my desk. From the kitchen pile, it moved to the top of a filing cabinet, and from there to a bookshelf in my office. One day, I pulled it out and added it to the stack of "things to do" in the basket on the corner of my desk. It stayed there another few months, before I finally opened it up and discovered the expired forms.

It took me months to fill them out. I'd open a document, type a single piece of information, then set it aside. A week or two later, I'd do a little bit more. Who am I? I kept asking myself. Who am I to ask to belong? I decided at least four times that I wasn't going to send the forms after all. And then, perhaps because I knew I'd spend the rest of my life carting that envelope around if I didn't, I finished the last document, signed it, and sent it all off to a government office on the other side of the country.

"You are now registered as an Indian ... in accordance with the Indian Act." The letter from Indigenous Affairs Canada had arrived on an otherwise normal day, while I was in the middle of cleaning the house. I sat down on the floor and sobbed. Attached to the letter was a temporary certificate of Indian status, to be followed by my card after I had supplied a photo, and a notification that I had been registered with my home band.

"Are you happy now?" I asked, half laughing, half crying, wondering if some ghost of my father might be lingering about, waiting on this dying wish to finally be fulfilled.

The answer came like a whisper, not in his voice but a dozen voices, a choir of ancestors that I know must have been imagined but felt real all the same: *Yes. Yes, we are happy now. We are very, very happy.*

...

The manager at my band office added me to a private Facebook group for off-reserve members. Community in the high-tech age. She posted a welcome, tagging me. I waited, fearful. I was an outsider, a stranger. Most of the people who knew my family when they still lived in that area might be elderly, or already gone. On top of that, I was registered under my married name, when my maiden name—the name I write with still—was the one that would identify me to others as kin. Why had I done any of this?

And then someone said hi, and sent me a private message: "We have the same great-granny," it read. Another one told me they'd grown up with my grandfather. Someone else said they remembered me from a holiday meal when they'd come to visit with their dad, my father's uncle. I'd worn an ivory dress with a blue bow, he recalled; I knew exactly which outfit he meant.

Most of the last names in the group were familiar to me, branches on my own family tree or names I had heard in stories my dad used to tell.

"It's so good to see the young ones finding their way home," someone posted a few weeks later, when another new member was welcomed.

It turned out that no one was mad that I was there, blond hair and all; they were happy I'd found my way back, that I'd found the path home, even if it had taken more than half my life.

To All the Crones I've Loved Before

To All the Crones I've Loved Before:

Thank you. For everything. Oh, wait. Hold on, back up. I should start with hello. Hello! And also: How are you? I hope you've been well.

I'm great. Really great. Mostly great. I mean, I'm great some of the time at least, and that's something, these days especially, right? Things have been a little wild here, and I know we've lost touch. I just wanted you to know I still remember everything you taught me. Everything, I promise.

I make my jerk chicken with that recipe you wrote on the back of the newsletter from your daughter's school, and my chai with the instructions you repeated to me three hundred times, give or take. I remember when you told me to be careful with my heart, and I wasn't, and you were right; I wish I could say I got more careful but I was always willing to risk a great deal, for love or desire.

You were my boss. And my co-worker, the one on the other side of the kitchen and later the one on the other side of a cubicle wall. The neighbour in that apartment building I hated so much, where the halls were dark and smelled of old cooking grease. You were the woman who intimidated me on the first day of my writer's workshop because you were so smart and accomplished and beautiful, but who, I didn't know until you told me much later, also felt uncertain and overwhelmed that very first day. You were my best friend's mom. My own mom. The mom I met at the pool who helped me when I had two little kids running in opposite directions while I tried to pull a bra onto my not-dry-enough body. You were the woman leading the group therapy, the one who squeezed my hand when I couldn't catch my breath for crying, and the woman in the seat next to me who had been where I was, just a few months before, and told me it would get better; I believed you, to my bones, and it was true. It did get better.

You were the one who showed me how to make a poultice (yes, people still do that) and how to make bread, and which herbs to plant in the sun and which in the shade. From you, I learned how to do the next right thing, and the next right thing and the next right thing, and to trust that the path will come together that way without worrying about where it is going. I learned from you how to hem a pair of pants and replace a button, and that a child with croup will often recover in minutes if you bundle them in a warm blanket and take them outside long enough to breathe the cold night air. Because of you, I learned a million things that I no longer remember learning but come to me when I need them, things I do without thinking, because that's the way you did them, like running a small knife around the edge of a canning jar to bump the bubbles and using the shampoo on the crown of my head and conditioner on the tips.

A few of you were already gone before I was born but I looked at your photos and imagined what you might tell me: when the salmonberries are ready for picking, maybe, which I never seem to get quite right, or how to cure an infant's colic with some long-forgotten kitchen remedy. So even though I never met you, still I need to say hello and thank you. And I miss you, which is perhaps a strange thing to feel about someone you've not met face to face, only spirit to spirit. But I do. I miss the chance to have known you, to have learned from you.

I would have called you a lot of things, in another time or another world: sister, auntie, mentor, elder, wise one, medicine woman, matriarch, queen. But in this life, I mostly call you friend, grateful that you (so many of you, a plural you, more than I deserved) crossed my path at all.

What would I have done without you? Lost myself in that man, lost myself in tears, lost myself in the furnace of postpartum depression. I wouldn't be able to make jerk chicken that's so good I lick the spicy sauce off the sharp blades of the blender the way some people lick cookie batter off the spoon. I wouldn't have known how to help a croupy baby (it works every time) or how to put in a tampon (aim slightly back, not straight up).

I wouldn't have found my way. I mean, I probably would have found my way, in the end—we all do somehow. But I'd have found it with a lot more bumbling and confusion and uncertainty. Your crone wisdom saved me, sent me in the right direction, laid down waypoints on the map, a path of candlelight to follow, one to the next, through the darkness.

How lucky I have been, to have you (all of you, each of you, sometimes for years at a time, sometimes for weeks or even days, sometimes only moments at a time, or only in imagined memories). Older and wiser is such a cliché but it's true—even when the older is only by a few years or months, and sometimes actually not older at all, just further along a particular path that is familiar to you but new to me.

I don't know when we forgot how much we need our crones. Somewhere between the Industrial Revolution and the Second World War. Sometime while the West was busy colonizing every place it could, bringing civilization to places that already had it in spades. Something to do with Hollywood, maybe, and *Vogue* magazine and companies that needed to sell us fear for the wrinkles and stretch marks that had once been markers of a valuable state of being. Sometimes I think it has something to do with Marilyn Monroe, who never had the chance to be a crone, who lives forever frozen in youthful perfection, a paean to womanhood.

I wish we had more crones. We need them. Because I realize now why we're all so scared of what's ahead: we forgot how important the crones are, especially the oldest of them. We convinced them to erase their aging, to stay young, but then we put them in homes when age caught up anyway. There wasn't room in our hectic daily lives for the slow-earned wisdom of crones. Who needs a grandmother to tell you what to do about colic when the internet is in your hand? We decided everything a crone had to tell us was an old wives' tale, pseudoscience, maybe even dangerous.

But did you know it was you that ensured humanity's survival? It's true, or at least it's a strong theory, and it makes sense to me: the crones made it possible for humans to have such a successful run at all, given how frail we are for the first many years of existence. A crone, finished raising her own offspring, could help protect and care for the children of her daughters. She could carry the memories and stories and recipes and medicines from an earlier generation. She could work on food acquisition and preparation. Basically, she did it all, her grey hair not a sign that she was past her usefulness but that she was, in fact, at the peak of it.

Imagine that. A crone who is at the centre of things, not shuffled to the side.

Anyway, I guess I'm rambling. I wanted to say thank you. And I promise to do my best to return the favour, to whoever needs it. To teach or share or listen. My crone years are just beginning but I hope that I will make them useful to the world—to help that young mom in the swimming pool like you helped me, to teach someone to plunge a knife around the edge of the pickled beets to bump the bubbles, to have the right words when a sister is broken-hearted (or at the very least, a cup of peppermint tea ready to go).

Most of all, I will do my best to remember that when the outward, physical signs of my aging feel like an invisibility cloak, that there is magic in being able to move, unseen, through the world.

All my love,
Christina (a forthcoming crone)

Beauty Tips for the End of the World

Retinol. Coenzyme Q10. Vitamin E. Peptides. Green tea extract. Glycolic acid. Lactic acid. Alpha hydroxy acid. All the acids.

The jars and tubes lining the shelf are glossy and bright, their packaging a rainbow of promises: this one will fix my laugh lines, this one my crow's feet, this one is for stretch marks, this one will lighten dark spots. But this one, this one right here in the silver and pink box, will tighten the skin on my neck. And this is what I came here for.

I put my hand to my neck, lift my chin to pull it taut, and let my fingers stroke up and down along the skin. It feels the same as it always has, but lately, in the right light and at the right angle, I've noticed it looks different. Rough. Loose. Crepey.

Crepey. What a horrible word, if it's even a word at all. I cannot think of a connotation in which we use this word that is pleasant. It's mostly reserved for women and their décolletage—another word I dislike, because I'm not sure how to pronounce it without sounding like an idiot and I don't really know how much of the body it refers to. Neck and clavicle? Upper chest only? All the way into the cleavage? French women know, I am sure, but I haven't a clue. All I know is that, once in a while, when I catch a reflection of myself by accident, my décolletage (regardless of its boundaries) looks *crepey*.

I pointed it out to my best friend a few days after I first noticed it.

"Uh, no, I don't really see it," she replied, a vague shrug of dismissal. I went and stood in the sunlight coming through the window and pulled my chin in like a turtle, knowing it would pucker the skin. "How about now?"

She rolled her eyes. "Well, yes, when you do that, it looks weird." I straightened up like an ostrich, neck long, extending my chin into the air, haughty. "Now?" She paused, bobbed her head back and forth, a motion that translates to "Well, maybe, but hard to say." I gave up asking for confirmation; it might not be obvious to anyone else yet, but it was obvious to me.

So, I need this cream. This cream will fix my neck, and then by domino effect, it will fix everything else in my life. That's how it works. The right face mask will solve dry skin and, in turn, solve everything else. The right zit treatment will clear up acne and, with it, all of life's problems. The right mascara will lengthen my lashes and turn me into a supermodel. This is the Law of Products: find the right one, in the prettiest package, and everything in your life could be perfect.

I know this is not true. This is only the magic of advertising, which I am too smart to be bamboozled by, too old to still be suckered. But I am, nonetheless, a little bit bamboozled and suckered. In that moment, with the expensive jar of miracle neck cream in my hands, the box still sealed and pristine, it seems like this promise of salvation—that I will be fixed with the right product—could be real.

I add the neck cream to my shopping basket, and continue down the aisle. I'm certain there's something else here that I don't know I need but will take my attention for a little while longer. I'm not yet ready to leave this place where perfect futures are still possible; I'm not yet ready to re-enter reality.

Reality is somewhere else, far away, something we watch through a screen. We tell ourselves this geographic and temporal lie: in a place that is definitely not here, definitely not now, there are floating islands of garbage in the ocean, and factories dumping toxic sludge into rivers where people swim. Fast fashion gets shipped from the other side of the planet, to be worn a time or two for an outfit-of-the-day reel on Instagram, and bagged up for donation; bundles of thin T-shirts and pre-ripped jeans then get shipped back overseas for resale in used fabric markets or turned to rags or simply get piled in a dump, often not far from where they were made in the first place.

Fancy tea bags deliver millions of microplastics into

your drink, and the ocean is full of them, too, thanks to face scrubs and synthetic fabrics and packing peanuts and the crappy plastic toy that came in the treat bag from the birthday party that your kid went to last weekend. The stuff you wash your car with is rinsed away into the nearby street drain and disappears into the local creek; next spawning season, there's half as many salmon.

Reality is a dread in my body that never really eases. It lingers, waiting for the middle of the night when I will lie awake knowing these problems are right here, right now, and believing myself solely responsible to both solve them and bear the burden of their guilt.

The air inside the drugstore starts to feel too cold after a while, a chill that prickles over my bare skin. Outside, it's "unseasonably warm," though I'm no longer sure we can call it unseasonable when each summer is hotter than the last. The longer I linger indoors with this shivery air conditioning, the more stifling my car will be upon return: the steering wheel will be too hot to touch, the belt buckles will burn if they touch bare skin. It's over thirty-five degrees Celsius outside now, in a region where twenty-seven is a warm summer day.

I pause in front of the shampoos. "Volume Intensity Max, with aloe and keratin." My eyes scan over the shampoo label of a brand I've not seen before, then on to the next one, checking prices and ingredients. A few are on sale; might be good to stock up. We always need more shampoo, more conditioner. I continue on, through tooth-paste. Dental floss. Band-aids. Heat pads. Vitamins.

Stuff. Endless rows of stuff. Everything in its own box, in plastic containers, manufactured out of materials I can't pronounce in countries I've never been to, shipped across the ocean, delivered in trucks to thousands of stores like this one, to millions of consumers who will use half the contents, then chuck the rest. The packaging will be discarded and who knows where it ends up: turned into something new, at best; shipped back overseas so someone else can deal with the problem at worst, the final invisible step in the endless conveyor belt of production and consumption.

For a moment, I'm overcome with the image of every-thing inside this store piled in a dump or washing up on beaches or filling street gutters or our water supply— discarded tongue scrapers and travel toothbrush covers and empty pill bottles dotting every landscape in the world. Outside, the world burns, and in here we shop for products we've been taught to believe are necessities.

I feel the weight of the cliché, the weight of my own fool-ishness even as I participate in it: to worry about one's neck is to be worried about aging and we are supposed to both age beautifully and not care about aging at all. I am supposed to be above that, by now. I was thirty when Nora Ephron wrote *I Feel Bad About My Neck*, and remember thinking that I, when the time came, would not. Feel bad about my neck, that is. I imagined we would evolve a great deal in the coming fifteen or twenty years. And in some ways, in collective ways, we have. But individually, and often silently, the next generation of women don't seem to feel so great about their necks, never mind their breasts, thighs, ankles, or tummies. If anything, we've been offered an ever-larger buffet of ways to fix ourselves over these last decades: your grandmother's bedside pots of cold cream have evolved into Brazilian booty lifts, CoolSculpting, Botox, collagen fillers. Forget your neck; feel bad about your aging labia? You can have those fixed, too. Just don't talk about it. You have to pretend none of it—aging or fixing the aging—is happening at all.

Vanity has always been both an expectation of and critique against women. You should care, but we'll mock you for admitting to it.

I grew up with the looming spectre of acid rain and the ozone hole: the first would kill us with water, the second with sun. More than a little terrifying, considering both are the basic necessities for life. We stopped using aerosols and talked about reducing air pollution, so less of the bad stuff would end up in the atmosphere. In the meantime, we cut up the plastic six-pack rings and adopted stretches of highway to keep them free from litter, and hoped for the best.

These days, we're all very pleased with ourselves when the blue recycling box is full of cardboard and plastic when we carry it to the curb on pickup day. Look how well we've done, taking care of the Earth, diligent in our recycling.

The goal should never have been a full blue bin. The goal should have been an empty one, reflecting lives in which we consume less—or better yet, a system that integrates solutions from the top down, in which the individual is no longer the only guilty party, frantically trying to recycle their way into a better world.

In lieu of that collective responsibility, most of us try to do what we can as individuals. My kids grew up on thrift-store and hand-me-down clothes. A third of my own wardrobe is second-hand, and a great deal of the new comes from local, sustainable, not-fast-at-all clothing companies. Much of the furniture in my house is ancient; I sit down to eat at the dining room table I grew up eating at. In the grocery store, I look for tin and glass in lieu of plastic, and every year our garden gets bigger so it can supply several months of produce that travels thirty metres rather than thousands of kilometres. We fix before buying new, doing the repairs ourselves when possible: I spent eight months with a jimmied-up starting mechanism on my washing machine to avoid replacing it. And when we finally did, we took the old one to a metal recycler. I make my own laundry detergent and buy handmade soap from a friend. As much as this reflects my worries, and the small ways I think I can mitigate my impacts, it also reflects privilege—the time and space and energy to think about these issues, along with just enough financial flexibility to have a few choices along the way.

...

In the magazine aisle, I scan the covers. Fashion trends. Yoga stretches. Beauty tips for the forty-plus set. What I really need is beauty tips for the end of the world. What to wear to the apocalypse. None of these magazines have such a thing, but I imagine it would say: skip the Botox and ignore the runway; it's time to disappear into the forest with a backpack of seeds.

As easy as this distraction is, I know a smooth neck will not save me from what is coming. A forehead free of wrinkles won't magic the microplastics out of the water supply or refreeze the disappearing glaciers.

I circle back to the beauty aisle and put the neck cream back on the shelf. Then pick it up again. Slide it back onto the shelf. Pick it up. I don't want to care about this, yet caring about it is such simple and seductive distraction, a habit formed by a lifetime of conditioning.

What difference will it make to the world if I buy it or don't buy it? What possible impact can I make now, here at the precipice, standing at the edge of the cliff and holding up my hands to stop the avalanche bearing down on me from above?

But what will I think of myself if I don't try, at least most of the time? If I don't attempt to wrestle with the garbage—literal and symbolic—and remember what is important and real, and what is not? I put the box back on the shelf a final time, pushing it with a fingertip back from the edge, and leave the store.

Reality is waiting.

The Last Couch I'll Ever Buy

My friend has been reading a book about "death cleaning." She tells me this while we're walking along a trail through a deep ravine and she pauses when she says it, using air quotes around the words.

"It's a whole thing. It's Swedish."

I've never heard of it before, but she explains the basic concept: you should minimize belongings, clean your home, and organize paperwork so that your death will be less of a burden on your children or other loved ones.

She has recently had a cancer diagnosis. It's one of the "good ones" that is solved with surgery, no additional chemo or radiation required. Still, its impact lingers, a question now raised that won't go away, a door that, once opened, can't be closed again.

I ask, with some hesitation, if she's reading it for herself, or out of general interest, though it strikes me as an odd choice to pick up at the bookstore just out of the blue.

"For me. And my parents, I guess. I mean, decluttering is good, even if you're not about to die."

She's not wrong, of course. I've been railing to my husband about a box of ancient hardcover *Popular Mechanics* encyclopedias in the attic with this exact argument: after we die, one of our kids will have to decide what to do with these, and then they will feel guilty about it, so why not deal with it right now?

He's in his early fifties, but seems to have no particular worries about his own mortality: death is a thing that will happen someday, down the road, and there's plenty of time to deal with a box of books, along with the old train tracks, a bunch of Meccano, and the yearbooks from his junior high school.

I envy this approach. I, on the other hand, fear that death may be lurking at any time, around the very next corner. It's a joke in my family that, among my siblings and me, it's not uncommon to answer the phone with a slightly breathy and panicked "What's wrong?" when someone calls, though the answer is almost always benign and there was no reason to think otherwise. Waiting for the other shoe to drop—or the first shoe to drop, for that matter—is a family trait, it seems.

"Maybe I should read it," I tell her. By now we're huffing back up a steep set of stairs to get to the upper lip of the ravine and back home. "Maybe I should have read it before this walk, actually." I laugh and gasp for breath, comically clutching at my chest. "Heart attack!"

She grimaces. A few years earlier, this same friend stood in the hallway of our gym, where I'd just stepped off the treadmill because I felt "weird," and insisted that I go see a doctor, which led to being taken by ambulance to the regional cardiac care centre.

I roll my eyes back in my head, pretend to gasp.

"Dude!" she says.

Okay, maybe not my best joke. But between the two of us, I figure we've earned our right to make jokes about death.

My mother was the first person I ever heard talk about "death buying"—not that she knew it, and not that death buying is "a whole thing" that a country, Scandinavian or otherwise, has enshrined into its cultural traditions.

"Well," she said, describing how she'd landed on a particular car when she bought a new one in her late sixties. "I chose something that I thought would last *long enough*. It's probably the last car I'll ever buy."

The last car she'd ever buy? I looked at her in surprise, frowning, scanning her from head to toe as though looking for some sign of injury or illness. Was something wrong? Was she sick? Was the other shoe about to drop?

But no. She was death buying, as I've come to think of it since: buying with her own future absence in mind.

"By the time this car starts giving out," she explained, "I'll be too old to drive anymore probably. Or ..." She shrugs, waving her hands in the air. "You know."

I did know. Or she'd be gone, she meant. She wasn't trying to be morbid or dramatic. In fact, just the opposite:

it was an entirely practical thing to decide what one might need with what remained of one's life. Why not choose accordingly?

But after the car, in the coming years, there were a growing array of purchases that were described as "the last one I'll ever buy." A new couch. A set of Le Creuset salt and pepper grinders. Expensive flannel sheets. On the plus side, after a life of necessary frugality (she wore the same coat the year I graduated high school as she had worn standing at the bus stop with me in kindergarten), she was finally more likely to indulge a little, to buy something "fancy" or known for its durability.

It was okay to spend a little bit more now, for quality. It had to last, after all. Not forever, of course—only until she wouldn't be here to need it.

For most of one's life, "stuff" is temporary. You buy new fluffy towels and you know that someday, you'll have washed the life right out of them and they'll start to fray and you'll cut them up and turn them into rags and then use those rags for a painting project one weekend and they'll be garbage. Dishes break, spoons get lost, books are borrowed by a friend and never returned. Toys are handed down to younger children, shoes lose their soles, luggage zippers break. Some things have a longer life cycle: clothes, if chosen wisely, can last years, through many seasons and trends and countless wearings. But they, too, will eventually thin and tear. Yes, a few objects will outlast us; we can imagine our jewellery going on to children or grand-children, and a solid hammer can be handed down over a few generations. But most of the goods that pass through our hands are short-lived in the grand scheme of things. We will always need another one, of whatever we've just bought, at some point.

Until one day we won't.

My mom is not the only one I know who is death buying. I've heard my mother-in-law, who is in her late seventies, describe things in this way. A friend of mine in his sixties, while shopping for a new coat, casually noted that if he got a good one, it'd probably last him the rest of his life.

In the last year or two, I've noticed it has started slipping into my own decision-making process. My couch is nearly twenty years old. It's a huge L-shaped sectional, far too large for the small living room it fills. But it was free and in good shape when it came to us as a hand-me-down from a family member who was downsizing. I put new foam inside the cushions a few years ago, and I've patched several rips in the fabric. One of the legs isn't even attached anymore, but is simply wedged between the couch and the floor to give the illusion of support. For most of the pandemic, my spouse turned it into his office, so there is now a curved divot in the seat that became his work-from-home "desk."

In other words, it is in desperate need of replacement.

But I have cats. And teenagers. And every time I think about buying something new, I pause: why not wait till the teenagers have become adults, and won't accidentally leave grilled cheese sandwiches between the cushions; why not hold off till the cats get old and lazy and stop using the corners as scratching posts?

And if I time it right, if I wait long enough, and choose something really sturdy, it might just be the last couch I'll ever buy.

An unexpected side effect of getting older is that you start measuring all sorts of decisions by laying them alongside your remaining time. How many books can I read in a year and how many years do I have remaining? Is it worth reading all the way to the end of a book that I'm not really enjoying, simply because someone deemed it important or it was a bestseller or all the smart people I know have recommended it? In my teens and twenties, I had a rule that if I started a book, I'd see it through. In my thirties, I was more likely to abandon a book unless required to finish it for some obligatory commitment; I suffered through every page of a novel that I loathed, because my whole book club was reading it and I knew I'd have to discuss it (and because it was so heavily lauded that I'd have felt stupid to confess I didn't adore it).

Now, if a book hasn't captured me in the first chapter, sometimes even the first five pages, it gets set aside and goes back to the library. I routinely take out a stack of ten or fifteen books and return most of them unread two weeks later. The librarians must think I'm a voracious reader with no other hobbies or commitments. But the reality is there isn't enough time left to read stuff I don't love, that doesn't feel necessary and urgent and valuable.

Travel, too, becomes defined by what your time will allow: it seems delightfully feasible to see dozens of countries when you're young (and the possibility of a lottery win is still ahead of you). Then one day you realize that you probably won't ever get to see India after all, and the chance you'll swim off the coast of Australia is shrinking year by year. There are only so many trips remaining that will fit your budget and the time span over which that budget must stretch. I am quite certain I will return several more times to my favourite local camping sites, or to the Gulf Islands, which are only a ferry ride away, and I am sure I'll see the far side of Canada at least one more time, if not two. But London? Miami? Tokyo? Maybe not.

Choices and experiences of all kinds begin to winnow: How many more amazing friendships will you foster? How many romantic partners might yet remain to be met? Can you still go back to school, change careers, change goals? Which of those great home-renovation projects will you get to? How about the hobbies you always wanted to take up, the things you wanted to learn? You can do some of them, of course. But you start to realize that the rest of your life—which once seemed like an endless banquet of days in which anything was possible—is a little more limited, year by year. And you have to start choosing: which of these possibilities is most important and which path will you take?

...

I have often believed there's enough inside of me for a hundred lives; enough to fall in love a hundred times, to happily settle down in a hundred places, pursue a hundred different passions, and see the sun set on a hundred different horizons. There's enough desire and want and curiosity inside of me, it seems, for maybe even a thousand lives. I understand now that the times I have felt most unhappy, most anxious, were the times when a choice had to be made, an entire fork in the road crossed off the map. Sometimes you can double back, try again, make a change, but not always. One kind of life precludes another, one choice limits all subsequent choices. The slow, dawning realization that every step I make is determining which one single life I will have to squeeze my existence into has been, at times, a hard revelation.

My husband once found me sitting inside the closet, a pile of Kleenex next to me, the tail end of a hard cry trailing off into hiccuping sniffles. He was frantic to understand the source, to figure out the problem and then solve it, hopefully with some kind of tool or glue or other practical hands-on repair.

But there was no way to explain it. How do you tell someone that you love this exact life you have—the one where you're sitting on the closet floor with a husband who is trying to figure out which screwdriver will fix whatever is broken, listening to your children down the hall play the same song on the recorder for the millionth time that day, with dishes piled in the sink from the food that fills your fridge, a bounty you know you are beyond privileged to have—while somehow grieving all the other lives you might have had, but won't?

It sounds selfish, the greedy wish of a child on their birthday who stomps their feet when there are not enough gifts to meet their expectations. But saying goodbye to the other versions of you that might have existed along a different set of choices is a kind of grief. At least for a little while.

There's a transition point when you are no longer young enough to believe your time will never run out and you're not quite old enough to be entirely pragmatic about the time that remains. That's where I am right now, in the in-between. Sure, I can joke about death cleaning and I can imagine that my next couch might be my final one, but I'm still getting comfortable with my mortality, still learning how to let go of the other possibilities my life might have held, still leaning into measuring what I most want against the time that remains.

But I understand a little more, month by month, year by year, the kind of peace that comes with not being afraid of the end, of knowing not just intellectually but in a bone-deep way that you will not, in fact, be the only person who ever lived who gets to skip out on the finale.

Creature from the Black Lagoon

It emerges from the edge of the lake, under moonlight: a glistening horror, dragging itself up on the shore to terrorize anyone in its path, a monster of slime and mud, dripping weeds in its wake. The heroine, making out with her beau in the backseat of a car parked at the lake's edge, narrowly escapes the monster's clutches, shiny curls bouncing as she scrambles backwards out of the car and onto the ground, a scream escaping her perfect, pouty, pink lips.

The monster is devouring the boyfriend, his lifeless form now sprawled across the seat. The heroine screams again and the monster looks up, spots its new target, renews its slow chase. The heroine runs as fast as she can, the click-clack of her heels echoing off into the distance as the monster lumbers along behind.

...

"Oh my god, the sweating. Like, you wake up just dripping."

"And the mood swings! Mad and then sad and then for a few minutes bliss—everything is amazing and you feel great—and then you're mad again. You want to break things. And then cry about it."

"And your period goes haywire. Hay. Wire. No period for months, then suddenly on the day you're leaving for a holiday, oh hi, it's your period again."

"Oh, don't forget the hair: chin hair and neck hair and I get one on my boob in the same place over and over; you don't even know they exist until the sun hits the bathroom mirror at just the right angle and boom—hair everywhere."

I'm sitting cross-legged on a friend's apartment floor in a circle of women. Everyone here is older than me by at least ten years, in some cases double that. In the midst of a conversation about writing and motherhood and sex and relationships and bodies, someone made a joke about meno-pause and I—at that point in my midthirties—squawked.

"No! Don't talk about it! I'm terrified," I said, laughing, arms up in mock protest. I grinned as I stuck my fingers in my ears and chanted, "Nanananananana, I can't hear you," to drown out their voices. I may have looked silly, but I wasn't exaggerating: menopause terrifies me. It is a monster that has lived in the back of my head for as long as I can remem-ber, its shadow always behind me, lurching ever closer with each birthday: the creature from the Black Lagoon come to terrorize in the night.

They ignore my protests entirely and proceed to

confirm that I am right to be afraid, with their endless list of complaints and maladies: the sweating, the mood swings, the haywire period, the chin hair, the hormones, the insomnia, and weight gain.

I grimace, look to the ceiling, and sigh with great drama.

"Aw, don't worry," someone says. "It passes." They all give reassuring nods. "And then, no more period!"

This does not sound like enough of a prize in exchange for everything that comes beforehand. "I guess so." Looking for the silver lining, I muster up a positive: "No more tracking your cycle to be sure you don't end up with a surprise baby every time you have sex."

"Oh, you won't care about sex. Seriously. I'm just not interested."

They debate this, too, all chiming in now, laughing and chuckling. One says she still likes the *idea* of sex but not so much the *reality* of it. Another, with more seriousness, points out that the hormone shift has made things more challenging "in the downstairs"—I interpret this to mean less moisture where there should be lots of moisture, but I don't really know. Another points out that men experience their own complications as they age, too—fewer erections where there should be lots of erections, I assume.

There is a general consensus that sex is overrated and exhausting.

"I could leave it or take it, and mostly I could leave it. It's not a big deal anymore," says the one closest in age to me.

I grimace, and frown, and I can feel my eyebrows coming together. It's impossible to keep my poker face.

"But, but ..." I don't know where to start. Sex *is* a big deal. I can't even fathom not caring about sex. I blather on. They chuckle. Someone pats me on the shoulder in comic sympathy. "That's the stage you're in *now*," someone else says. "How old are you? Yeah, sexual peak. It'll pass."

I don't want it to pass. I don't want to worry about my downstairs problems—or those of a partner's. I don't want chin hairs or mood swings. I don't want to wake up in sweat-soaked blankets. I don't want to be old. All of it sounds hideous. Monstrous.

And that's when I realize, sitting there on the floor, in between bites of hummus and crackers, with a gorgeous spring breeze coming through the window and the laughter of my friends in the air: The monster isn't chasing me. I am the monster.

If I'm running away, it's from my own frightening, future self.

The monster never seems to tire, or slow down. It lurches, step after step, in a slow-motion chase, along a dark stretch of highway. When cars pass, it hides in the shadows, invisible, waiting to continue. It doesn't matter how far the heroine runs, how many times she screams for help, the monster will catch up, eventually.

"The change of life." That's what my mother called it, or simply "the change." My mother is a pragmatic woman:

time passes, children grow up, bodies age. That's just how it goes. The alternative is not being here at all. So whatever the passage of time brings you—an empty nest, wrinkles, slowing down—there's no solution but to accept it.

And I don't recall that her experience of menopause was particularly bad. Though perhaps it's more accurate to say that she didn't talk about it much and I, prone to worrying about things that are still far away if I know too much about them, simply didn't ask for details. Like a toddler, if I can't see it, maybe it won't exist. Even now, I still haven't asked for specifics. Every time I think about doing so, I hesitate. Next month, I think. Next year.

We inherit a great deal from our mothers, genetically and emotionally, but this fear of menopause did not come from my mom. Now that I think about it, she might be one of the only sources of information in my life that didn't imply I ought to fear what was coming. Because everything else—film, television, books, magazine articles—all comes with the same message: the worst sins a woman can commit are to be fat or old, or both, and menopause is a sure marker of the latter and often comes with the former, if you weren't already. All one needs to do is stand in the magazine aisle, or flip through daytime talk shows, to encounter this long-held truth: menopause will be awful and you will be diminished by it.

I have been steeped in this message, and absorbed it by osmosis, for most of my life.

...

Each time it seems like the monster has been avoided, it reappears. The heroine hides in an alley, but it doesn't take long for the monster to sniff her out. She finds the sheriff, and he heads off to save the day; off-screen, we hear a gunshot, then a scream of fear, then silence. The monster's shadow looms in the light of the street lamp, still in pursuit. The heroine is exhausted and alone. She won't be able to carry on much longer.

On a five-hour drive from Vancouver to the interior of BC, I listened to the audiobook of *The Menopause Manifesto* by Dr. Jen Gunter. I'd found Gunter on social media, a one-woman army defeating misinformation about the female body and fighting misogyny wherever it might be found. I hadn't read her earlier book, *The Vagina Bible*, but when I made a joke about perimenopause on Facebook one day, a half dozen women had urged me to check out *Manifesto*.

For the full five hours of the drive, I hooted with laughter, I cried several times, I nodded in agreement or sighed in exasperation. More than once I shouted "Yes, exactly!" or "What? I had no idea!" into the empty car. I kept wishing I had other people there with me to dissect it all as it unfolded, pressing pause so we could hash out what we'd just heard. It was a metaphorical and, at times, literal jaw-dropper.

The sad truth was that I learned more about my body in five hours than I had in an entire lifetime of living in it.

Facts. Statistics. Myths. Medicine. I heard basic biological facts about puberty and pregnancy and perimenopause that I'd somehow never encountered, despite having lived through the prior two stages already.

But the passages that stayed with me the most? The ones that suggested that older women in particular were crucial to the success of humankind, a theory I'd never heard before.

Post-menopausal women, Gunter explained, were likely a critical component for the survival of the early human species. When you've got offspring that take years to be self-reliant, a grandmother is a very useful addition. With her own children now grown, a grandmother is free to help with the next generation. She is also extra hands for food production, extra eyes for safety, extra wisdom for teaching. In other words, women who were beyond their own reproductive years were what made the next generation's reproductive years successful. Multiply that by thousands of generations and grandmothers, and you've got one part of the puzzle that allowed humans to not just survive but thrive.

For the first time, I had a different kind of message to absorb. One that was not just positive, but revolutionary: the idea that a woman past her prime might not be "less than" she was before; if anything, she is probably *more*.

The heroine races for home, dashing up the steps and through the door. She doesn't think about the fact that she's cornered now, that by hiding in the basement she's removed any chance of escape. The creature has arrived. *Thump thump thump*, on the floorboards above the heroine's head, then pausing at the basement door, then *thump thump thump* down the stairs.

The monster sits down in the old armchair, leans back and sighs.

"It's so good to be home," the monster says. When the heroine sneaks a peek between her fingers, the monster is pulling off its mask: layers and layers of stereotypes and clichés and assumptions. It's like looking into a mirror; the monster could be her twin, but older, with salt and pepper hair, laugh lines at the corners of her eyes. Not at all scary, the heroine realizes. In fact, the monster is beautiful.

"It's good to have you here," says the heroine, a little shy, but mostly relieved. This isn't, she realizes, the end. It might actually be the beginning. "Tea?"

What Comes After

Every week or two, a new version of myself shows up at the doorstep, waiting to be welcomed in. She makes her presence known in different ways: loud obvious knocks, gentle taps, a singsong hello—a milestone birthday, a sudden shift in thinking, small physical changes. Each one is a little bit different than the one who came before, and different again than the one who will arrive next.

I used to believe this process—of aging, of watching myself age, of moving into this unfamiliar territory alongside friends who are aging themselves—would come easy to me. I was certain that midlife would be simple, calm, relaxing even. Smack dab between the uncertainties of the first act of my life but with the big finale still far off in the distant future, this would be a place to stop, sit back, and exhale. I figured I'd be gracious and welcoming to this ever-older, ever-wiser version of myself who looked and thought like me but also not at all like me. I'd be grateful, and good-humoured, and unbothered.

And sometimes I am. In public, I try to be. I make comical posts on Facebook about chin hairs and the joys of mammograms, and chuckle with friends over knees that don't function as they did twenty years ago. I get weepy about the transitions of parenting, but find ways to celebrate the renewed independence I experience now that my children are no longer little. I lean into the stability and certainty of my life, still marvelling that I somehow managed to figure things out along the way.

But when it's just me, by myself, staring in the mirror? Or waiting in a doctor's office for a test result? Or lying in bed thinking about which paths I took, and which I have left unexplored? I am not very gracious or grateful at all. I am mostly scared that time, just when I need it to slow down, seems to be speeding up, and irritated with the unwelcome visitors from my own future who continue to arrive.

The algorithm has really figured me out. My social media feeds are full of ads for supplements to balance my hormones, handheld infrared devices to minimize crow's feet, products to ease hot flashes, along with reels from "aging" content creators. I get videos about mobility exercises, and makeup reviews featuring age-spot concealer. I am at once horrified by and drawn to all of it: I don't feel old enough to be included in the target demographic, yet

I'm compelled by the content because I am, absolutely, the target demographic.

I was quite certain that the resistance to aging I heard others express when I was younger was tied up in the individual and driven by their own vanity: how each person feels about themselves and that first grey hair, the wrinkles that appear around their eyes, the way their bodies change as they age. It's the grief and loss of "what was"— beauty, desirability, the power that these can bestow. This is where I would excel at aging, I told myself, because you can't grieve the disappearance of something you've not had.

I grew up in the era of the supermodel. I recall Farrah Fawcett's iconic red-bathing-suit poster gracing the bedroom walls of older cousins, and pictures of Kate Moss, ripped from *Vogue* and *Vanity Fair*, taped up inside friends' lockers as we prepared to graduate from high school. Fawcett was thin, fun, and feminine; Moss was a waif, moody and brooding, a modern twist on the starving-ballerina aesthetic popular a decade earlier. Between these bookends was Cindy Crawford, whose career dominated my adolescence: big hips, big breasts, and big hair. In reality, only the hair was big; the rest of her was big compared to other models, not the women I saw around me. She wasn't even all that tall, coming in at five foot nine, but she was the biggest girl on the catwalk. There was no such thing yet as Ashley Graham or Yumi Nu. In fact, the only plus-sized models I ever saw were the sturdy little boys in the "husky" section of the Sears catalogue.

The options presented to me—Farrah, Kate, Cindy—
were unobtainable. Discovering early on that I didn't meet
the prerequisites was paralyzing, creating deep insecurities
that guided my behaviours for years. But it was also, ultimately, freeing. If I wasn't up to snuff, if I didn't or couldn't
please others, I needed only to please myself. In that case,
how could aging undermine me? If I had never had audience approval, the only approval that counted when the
time came would be my own.

It turns out I severely underestimated the collective influence
of, well, the entire world—and overestimated my ability to
observe from afar, intellectually detached, as though I was
uninvolved. Ageism doesn't wait until you cross some particular number of birthdays before it affects your actions or
the way you're perceived by others or yourself. Disdain for
aging—aging as a woman in particular—reaches its tendrils
out to everyone, at every prior stage of life, feeding a fear of
what's to come long before it arrives. The cure for this, we
learn, is to avoid being seen to be aging at all.

I didn't particularly follow *Sex and the City* in its first incar-
nation, but I somehow ended up watching the movie about
a dozen times during my second pregnancy and my first
few months post-partum: it was light and easy, and full of
pretty clothing to admire and friendships that were vicariously supportive and cheerful. When the reboot launched,
despite the heavy criticisms of the show, I eventually binged
the first season: still lots of pretty clothes and supportive

friendships, plus fancy restaurants and gala events. With my attention span at low capacity after a few years of COVID-19, it was—despite the warranted criticism—an easy watch and a low-stakes escape from suburban life.

It was also, I realize now, my brain's way of considering what was ahead: If they had reached midlife, so had I, and that was okay. If they were talking about age and wrinkles and menopause, managing changed relationships and juggling teenagers and dealing with unexpected deaths and the shifting of identity, it seemed all the more reasonable that I could be, too (albeit in not quite so stylish clothing or lavish surroundings).

But where I saw myself on that screen most readily, most ashamedly, was in the second season, when Carrie is invited to help launch a new magazine aimed at older women. She balks, horrified to have been included, dismayed at the discovery that others might consider her a visible and obvious member of the demographic.

As embarrassed as I was for her fictional behaviour, I was more ashamed of my own real-world reaction. Her fear of being considered "in-group" when she saw herself as "out-group"—and the uncertainty of not knowing which category the rest of the world was placing her in—was a mirror of my own internalized ageism. I was doing the same thing and had been for years, drawing circles around who belonged where. Yes, I'm *almost there*, I'd tell myself, but I'm not *there yet*. Because *there*, I've been assured, is going to be scary and unpleasant and something, certainly, to fear.

...

No matter how you dress, or what you do, much of a woman's life is spent standing in the centre of a stage under spotlights, an object on display, something to be observed, open to scrutiny or praise, desire or rejection, comment and critique. We become so accustomed to the spotlight that it's impossible to imagine life without it. We are taught to fear the loss of it: someday you will be shuffled off, expected to exit stage left, where you may watch from the wings. Rest assured, the warning continues, this will be a state of loss and abandonment and isolation.

This last decade, as I learned to love myself in ways I never had before, saw beauty where I thought none existed, began to live and dress and behave to meet my own expectations and not everyone else's, I didn't realize how much power the stage still had, how much the shape of me was defined by an audience I pretended not to care about.

Most of us would not choose the spotlight that comes with being a woman in this world, but we have become so accustomed to it that performing is second nature. Who are you if, and when, you stop? Who are you when no one is looking?

I've been a terrible host so far. These new versions of myself that keep showing up at the door are given a luke-warm reception, a feigned embrace, a show of welcome. They make me nervous, asking me to re-evaluate how much I care, and about what, and why. I can sense they have less need to please, and an urgency to heed their own opinions and desires. They haven't forgotten about the audience—I don't think they ever will—but they've begun to turn their backs. They're not afraid of what happens next, offstage; they've seen the exit that is waiting behind the curtain. I only have to follow their lead and trust that maybe, just maybe, what comes after was never something to fear at all.

Afterword:
The Other Side of the Forest

The thing about a long journey is that everything you bring with you for the trip will change, and sometimes fall apart, as you go. The soles of your shoes wear thin, the wagon wheel breaks, you run out of matches. Along the way, you acquire new tools and supplies, out of necessity or luck. You come across a beehive dripping honey, and take some with you for the road. You realize you need a bigger wagon, or none at all. The axe that has become dull needs sharpening, or you trade it for a new one.

You change, too. Your legs get stronger day by day. You learn to recognize the sounds in the forest, which noises to ignore and which require caution. You figure out when to rest and when to keep going. And just as you decide you finally know the lay of the land, the geography changes: You head up into the mountains, or drop down into a valley. Food gets scarce, or plentiful. The weather turns when you're least expecting it.

Nothing stays the same. And nothing can be predicted with any accuracy. There's no alternative but to keep going, knowing that some of what you have, and some of what you know, will be useful on the road ahead—and some of it will mean nothing at all, or may even slow you down if you don't leave it behind.

You'll cross paths with people who have already been where you're going and they'll have advice—or warnings—that may or may not be wise or real or necessary. Take everything with gratitude, grace, and a grain of salt. You might, if you're lucky, come across fellow travellers heading in the same direction, and a few of these, the best ones, will make good companions for the trip.

Either way, you'll know more in the middle of the journey than you did at the beginning—and you'll also know that whatever is ahead, you'll have to learn it, solve it, figure it out, and get through it, just as you have until now: one step at a time.

I have glimpses of what's on the other side of the forest, what's around the next big bend in the trail, on the other side of that peak. But I've learned there's no such thing as a map that is finished.

And the map of this journey—of life, and how to navigate it—will be a work in progress for the rest of my days, as it is for each of us. Most of the path ahead will be a mystery, until it's not.

I do know one thing for sure now though: the more you share your map, and others share theirs with you—filling in the blanks for each other, describing the valley

you've already been through, the field they passed by—
the easier the path will be for both of you. The best way,
maybe the only way, to get to the other side of the forest
is together.

We're halfway home, my friends, but we are not alone.

Acknowledgements

As I write these words, I am bursting with gratitude; I could fill a hundred pages with thanks to teachers and mentors and friends and family, to the people I've worked with in loud kitchens and busy newsrooms, and to those who have been alongside me in so many ways, writing or otherwise.

The short practical version, in lieu: with endless thanks to my husband, who is not so great at folding laundry but is perhaps the world's leading expert at being supportive of other people's dreams, which makes for messy laundry rooms but a loving marriage; and my children, who have never complained about the hours I spend "working on something" even when it has meant that dinner is late and comprises half a watermelon and some hot dogs.

Also, to my siblings for, well, everything. And Mom for letting me talk and talk and talk. And my extended clan of family and in-law family, who show up in so many ways.

And big love for my bestest cheerleaders. You know who you are, but just in case, specifically: my middle-of-the-night-crisis besties; the Foxy Nerds; the not-really-but-kind-of-a-coven; the best pen pal in the history of the universe; the pandemic-survival friends; my writing twinsie; and finally, the entire TWS community.

I am thankful, as well, for the support of the British Columbia Arts Council for this project, and to the BC writing community and the many writers in this province from whom I have found so much inspiration and mentorship.

With so much gratitude to my agent, Emmy Nordstrom Higdon, for their magic and enthusiasm, and the team at Westwood Creative Artists, along with my editor Shivaun Hearne, for seeing in this book what I wanted to create, and everyone at House of Anansi for bringing it to life.

And most of all, to readers, without whom we'd all just be shouting stories into the wind for an audience of trees and flowers and wild bunnies: thank you for still being here.

An earlier version of "The Pencil Test" was published in the anthology *Boobs: Women Explore What It Means to Have Breasts*, edited by Ruth Daniell (Caitlin Press, 2016).

In the essay "This Necessary Amnesia," the lines from Kahlil Gibran's "On Children" are from *The Prophet* (Knopf, 1923). This poem is in the public domain.

An earlier version of "What Were We Thinking?" was published in *Asparagus* magazine in July 2022.

© Wendy Lees

CHRISTINA MYERS is a writer, editor, and former journalist. Her novel *The List of Last Chances* (2021) was longlisted for the Leacock Medal for Literary Humour, shortlisted for the Fred Kerner Book Award, and won the fiction category of the Canadian Book Club Awards. She edited the award-winning anthology *BIG* (2020), and her work has appeared in anthologies, magazines, and newspapers. An alumnus of the Writer's Studio at Simon Fraser University, she now teaches creative writing through SFU's continuing studies program. She is a parent of teens, a garage-sale treasure hunter, an enthusiastic but terrible gardener, a fan of dresses with big pockets, and perhaps best of all: a forthcoming crone. She is a member of Da'naxda'xw First Nation, though grew up all over Canada, and now lives in Surrey, British Columbia. Find her online at cmyers.ca.